Georgia Test Power

Grade 4

ISBN   978-0-544-21271-8

1 2 3 4 5 6 7 8 9 10   2266   22 21 20 19 18 17 16 15 14 13

4500428449   A B C D E F G

Contents

Introduction

What Is the *Georgia Test Power* Book?

The *Georgia Test Power* book is a workbook that helps you prepare to take the CRCT as well as transition to taking the PARCC tests of the Common Core State Standards. The questions in these tests are based on the skills you learn in school.

The Reading Practice Test in this book tests your reading and language arts skills. For some questions, you will read passages and answer questions about them. For other questions, you will read writing and answer questions about how to make the writing better. The Writing Practice Tests have you analyze and write in response to one or more texts. Reading/Writing Practice Tests have you read stories and articles and write answers to questions about them.

How to Use this Book

This book includes reading, language arts, and writing lessons. The reading lessons review skills that help you understand different kinds of reading material. The language arts and writing lessons review information important to helping you meet the Common Core State Standards.

You will get the most out of the reading experience if you ask yourself questions as you read:

- What is the passage mostly about?
- What do I already know about this topic?
- Is the passage making sense to me?
- Which parts do I need to reread?
- What can I do to understand words that I do not know?
- What did I learn from the passage?

You will get the most out of the language arts and writing experience if you do the following:

- Think about a plan before you write.
- Make a first try at the writing.
- Think about ways to make the writing better.
- Make changes to improve the writing.
- Think about citing sources and text details in your writing.

Learning to read and write well is like learning to ride a bike. The more you practice, the easier it becomes. Before you know it, you are riding with ease. So, let's hop on and get started!

Story Structure

How to Analyze the Text

The story *Because of Winn-Dixie* takes place in a small town in Florida, probably during the 1960s. It is important that the story is set there and then so that Opal can have the experiences that she does.

The **setting** of a story is the time and place in which the story happens. To identify the setting of a story, ask yourself these questions:

- Where do events in the story happen?
- When do events in the story happen?

Thinking carefully about a story's setting can help you understand why events in the story happen the way they do. Suppose you read a story about a brother and sister who spend the night in a campground. The fact that the children sleep in the woods at night will affect the events and characters in the story.

The **plot** is the story line, or the events that happen. The events in one part of a story influence what happens later. A careful reading of the plot will help you identify which events in one part affect the events in a later part. The plot also helps you understand the conflict, or main problem, in the story and how the characters try to solve the conflict. The way the problem is solved is called the resolution or solution.

When you read a story, asking the following questions will help you understand the plot:

- How is the problem finally solved?
- How does the character try to solve the problem?
- How do events in the story influence other events?
- What is an important problem for a character in the story?

GO ON ▶

Name _____ Date _____

Apply to Text

Read the passage below and answer the questions that follow.

The Golden Reed Pipe

(A Folktale from China)

1   Long ago in China, there lived a woman and her daughter. The daughter was called Little Red because she always wore red clothing.

2   One day, Little Red and her mother were plowing and sowing the fields. There was a fierce wind, and then a dragon swooped down! He grabbed Little Red and carried her away. Her mother heard Little Red's voice crying:

Oh mother, oh mother, as dear as can be,

My brother, my brother will rescue me!

3   The poor mother did not know what to think. She had no son, so Little Red had no brother. The woman was upset as she walked home and did not see the large tree. Her hair became tangled in the trees branches which she noticed had bright red berries. After she untangled herself, she saw a lost little boy under the tree. She brought the boy to live with her and named him Redberry.

4   Redberry was outside one day when he heard a crow cry:

You have a sister out there, out there!

Save her from the dragon's lair!

5   Redberry had no idea he had a sister! He ran to his mother, who told him about Little Red and what had happened. The boy was so angry at the dragon that he set out to rescue his sister. He walked for miles and miles in search of the dragon's lair. Then he came to a large rock that was blocking his way. He rolled the rock away and found a shiny golden reed pipe.

6   When Redberry blew on the pipe, he saw movement out of the corner of his eye. Then he realized that all the frogs and other creatures were dancing. The faster he played the tune, the faster they danced.

7   "Aha!" cried Redberry. "I know just what to do! Now I can deal with the dragon!"

8   When he came to the dragon's cave, he saw a girl
     dressed in red and knew it was his sister. He also saw a
     dragon. The dragon was scarier than Redberry expected.

9   Redberry blew on the pipe, and the dragon began to
     dance. The faster Redberry played, the faster the dragon
     danced. At last the dragon cried:

     I'll send her home

     If you leave me alone!

10   Redberry knew better than to believe a dragon. He led
     Little Red·and the dragon away from the cave. He kept
     on playing until they came to the sea. With a splash, the
     dragon fell in! Then the sister and brother returned home
     hand-in-hand. They both came to their mother, who cried
     with joy.

> **Look Closely**
>
> How is the conflict resolved?
> How do things turn out for the
> characters?

1   **How can you tell that this is a folktale and not realistic fiction? Use evidence
     from the text to support your answer.**

     _____

     _____

     _____

     _____

2   **What is the MAIN problem the woman and Redberry face in the folktale?
     Use text evidence to support your answer.**

     _____

     _____

     _____

     _____

GO ON ▶

3 Think about how the author organized information in the folktale.

Complete the timeline with ONE important detail from the folktale.

| A dragon carries Little Red away. | → | Redberry goes to find Little Red. | → | | → | The dragon falls into the sea. |

Explain why this detail is important. Use evidence from the text.

_____

_____

_____

_____

_____

4 How is the problem in the folktale resolved? Give TWO details from the folktale to support your answer.

_____

_____

_____

_____

_____

STOP

Author's Purpose

How to Analyze the Text

In the selection *My Brother Martin,* Dr. Martin Luther King Jr.'s sister reflects on growing up with Dr. King. Her purposes for writing are to describe her experiences and to inform readers about Dr. King.

Authors write for different **purposes**, or reasons. Some purposes that authors have for writing are to describe, to entertain, to explain, to inform, and to persuade. An author often has one clear purpose. Other times an author writes for more than one purpose.

Authors do not usually state why they are writing. It is up to the reader to figure it out, using clues in the selection. Read the chart below to learn more about identifying an author's purpose.

Author's Purpose	Features of the Reading Selection	Examples
To describe	Words that tell how things look, sound, smell, or taste	Essay, letter, magazine article, poem
To entertain	Tells about characters or people and the events in their lives May make readers feel happy, scared, or sad	Play, poem, story
To explain	Gives directions Explains how something works or why something happens	Directions, magazine article, newspaper article
To inform	Gives facts and information	Report, newspaper article, magazine article
To persuade	Tries to get reader to agree with the author Gives beliefs and opinions	Advertisement, book review, letter

GO ON ▶

Name _____ Date _____

Apply to Text

Read the passage below and answer the questions that follow.

Land of Fire and Ice

1   Would you like to visit a land where you can see
things that are both very hot and very cold? Iceland is
a country that has both volcanoes and glaciers. That is
why the country is called the "Land of Fire and Ice."

2   Iceland is about the size of the state of Virginia. Still, it
has more hot springs and volcanoes than any other country
in the world. There are about 200 volcanoes, which makes
Iceland one of the busiest volcano areas on Earth. A
volcano erupts in this tiny area about every five years! In
1963, a volcano erupted and made a brand new island.
Within four years, because of more eruptions, this island
grew to an area of 1 square mile. The island soon rose to
more than 560 feet above sea level.

Look Closely

This passage includes many
facts. Think about how giving
facts relates to the author's
purpose.

3   Glaciers are another part of Iceland. Glaciers are
large, slow-moving masses of ice and snow. Some of the
largest glaciers in the world are in Iceland, and much
of Iceland is covered with glaciers. In fact, more than
10 percent of Iceland is covered with glaciers. Only
Antarctica and Greenland have bigger ones.

4　Iceland lies just below the Arctic Circle. It is warmer, though, than you might think. The waters of the Gulf Stream in the Atlantic Ocean keep Iceland warm. The average July temperature is a very comfortable 51°F. Of course, in winter Iceland gets much colder.

Look Closely

What is the author telling you? Why?

5　Only about 321,000 people live in Iceland. Most people live in Reykjavik, the capital. They still speak the same basic language as the Vikings who first settled the island. The Vikings, who journeyed by boat from Scandinavia, began settling in Iceland more than a thousand years ago.

6　Icelanders enjoy nature activities. The beautiful and interesting geography attracts visitors who like the outdoors. For all people who enjoy nature at the extreme, Iceland is a paradise of fire and ice.

Look Closely

In this paragraph, the author gives an opinion. What does the author want you to think?

1　What is the MOST LIKELY reason the author wrote this passage?

　A　to explain how to travel to Iceland

　B　to inform readers about Iceland's geography

　C　to persuade readers that Iceland is very cold

　D　to entertain readers with stories about Iceland

GO ON

2   **Which clues in the passage BEST help to identify the author's purpose?**

     A   facts about Iceland

     B   stories about the Icelandic people

     C   details about how Iceland sounds and smells

     D   explanations about how volcanoes and glaciers form

> **Look Closely**
>
> Look for details, such as facts (inform), sensory details (describe), opinions (persuade), or feeling words (entertain) that suggest why the author wrote the passage.

3   **Why do you think the author MOST LIKELY chose the title "Land of Fire and Ice"?**

     A   to frighten and excite readers

     B   to explain how Iceland got its name

     C   to prevent readers from visiting Iceland

     D   to stress Iceland's most interesting features

> **Look Closely**
>
> The title can help you understand why the author wrote the passage.

4   **What is the MAIN purpose of Paragraph 3?**

     A   to inform readers about glaciers in Iceland

     B   to entertain readers with stories about glaciers

     C   to explain why Iceland is covered with glaciers

     D   to persuade readers that Iceland has the best glaciers

> **Look Closely**
>
> Paragraph 3 gives facts about Iceland's glaciers. Think about why the author gives facts instead of opinions or detailed descriptions.

2 Ⓐ Ⓑ Ⓒ Ⓓ

3 Ⓐ Ⓑ Ⓒ Ⓓ

4 Ⓐ Ⓑ Ⓒ Ⓓ

STOP

Cause and Effect

How to Analyze the Text

The selection *My Librarian Is a Camel* tells about the different ways that people deliver books to children living in the world's most faraway places. These moving libraries have a wonderful effect on the children they serve. They deliver happiness along with the books, and they get the children excited about reading.

Authors can connect ideas or events by using cause and effect. A **cause** is a reason that something happens. An **effect** is what happens as a result of the cause.

To understand cause and effect, ask yourself what happened (effect) and why it happened (cause). As you read, look for words and phrases that might signal a cause-and-effect pattern. These words include *as a result, because, since, so,* and *therefore.*

Sometimes an author first explains what happened (effect) and then explains why it happened (cause). Other times the author tells about the cause and then the effect. In some stories, an event can be both an effect of something that has happened and a cause of something else that will happen. Then the series of causes and effects is like a game of tag.

Cause	Effect/Cause	Effect
Ana tags Josh.	Josh is *It*.	Josh tags Ben.

Sometimes a cause can have more than one effect.

A drought, or lack of rain (cause), can cause grass to turn brown, ponds to dry up, and crops to not grow (effects).

Sometimes an effect has more than one cause.

The school fair was a great success (effect) because the food was delicious, there were many new games and prizes, and more people than ever showed up (causes).

GO ON

Name _____ Date _____

Apply to Text

Read the passage below and answer the questions that follow.

Two Endangered Animals

1   Around the world, more than a thousand animals are endangered. If an animal is endangered, it may soon become extinct. There are two animals that scientists fear are disappearing quickly. These animals are the rhinoceros and the giant panda. The threat to these animals grows larger every day, and the time to save them is running out. Extinction is not reversible.

Look Closely

Look for what happens (the effect) and why it happens (the cause).

2   A major threat to these endangered animals is the loss of habitat. A habitat is the area in which an animal lives. Habitats are being changed or damaged worldwide. As a result of losing their habitats, animals can no longer find food or places to live. Hunting and poaching also threaten endangered animals. Poachers are those who kill an animal illegally. They may kill it for sport or for parts of its body.

The Rhinoceros in Danger

3   The rhinoceros is an amazing animal. It has lived on Earth since prehistoric times. One of the largest animals in the world, rhinoceroses have short legs but huge bodies. Some rhinoceroses can weigh two tons! A rhinoceros has one or two horns. The horn, which grows out of its nose, is used for protection. Rhinoceroses live in Africa and southeastern Asia.

4   The rhinoceros has nearly disappeared for many reasons. First, since more people are living on its land, the rhinoceros is losing its natural habitat. Another reason is that many people in Asia use the rhinoceros horn for medicine. As a result, poachers kill rhinoceroses just for their horns.

Look Closely

Look for signal words such as *because, as a result, since,* and *so* to identify cause-and-effect relationships.

Saving the Rhinoceros

5   Many countries are working as fast as possible to save the rhinoceros. Countries have laws making it illegal to hunt the rhinoceros. Some countries have areas of land in which the rhinoceros's habitat is protected. For instance, most rhinoceroses in Zimbabwe have been moved to nature preserves that are guarded and surrounded by high fences.

Giant Pandas at Risk

6   Giant pandas live in China. They live on high mountain slopes and eat bamboo. These cute black-and-white animals look like giant teddy bears. They can grow to be 5 or 6 feet tall and can weigh 200 to 300 pounds.

7   Like the rhinoceros, the giant panda is facing several real dangers that may cause it to become extinct. First, many of the forests in which giant pandas once lived have been cut down for farming and lumber. Therefore, many giant pandas live without shelter. Second, some bamboo forests aren't growing because of lack of rain. This often causes giant pandas to starve. Finally, because the fur of the giant panda is highly valued, poachers are killing giant pandas for their fur.

> **Look Closely**
>
> In some cases, an effect may have several causes. Look for words that identify several causes of one effect, such as *first* and *second*.

Protecting the Giant Panda

8   The Chinese government has set aside protected land for giant pandas. However, unlike the rhinoceros, the giant panda needs a large area of land on which to live. This is because the giant panda needs massive amounts of bamboo to survive.

9   For the rhinoceros and the giant panda, not much time is left. There are fewer places for them to live. Fortunately, scientists are continuing to work with countries to find solutions to these problems.

GO ON ▶

Name _____ Date _____

1   Why is the rhinoceros in danger of extinction?

   A   It has many natural predators.

   B   It is hunted by poachers and is losing its natural
        habitat.

   C   It can no longer grow horns to protect itself.

   D   The giant panda is taking its land.

Look Closely

Reread Paragraph 4. Which of
these matches the causes in
the passage?

**2   What is an effect of the giant panda becoming
      endangered?**

   A   More and more people are hunting the giant panda
        for its fur.

   B   It doesn't have enough bamboo to eat.

   C   The Chinese government has set aside land for the
        giant panda.

   D   It is losing its habitat.

3   What happens when an animal becomes extinct?

   A   The animal is gone from the Earth forever.

   B   The animal can be brought back once its habitat
        is restored.

   C   The animal becomes endangered.

   D   Hunters can continue to hunt the animal.

Look Closely

Not all causes and effects
are directly stated. Look at
Paragraph 1 to figure out the
effect of extinction.

**4   Which of these is NOT a cause for giant pandas to
      be endangered?**

   A   There is not enough rain in the
        bamboo forests.

   B   Poachers hunt pandas for their fur.

   C   The forests are disappearing.

   D   Pandas live too far apart from
        each other.

1 Ⓐ Ⓑ Ⓒ Ⓓ

2 Ⓐ Ⓑ Ⓒ Ⓓ

3 Ⓐ Ⓑ Ⓒ Ⓓ

4 Ⓐ Ⓑ Ⓒ Ⓓ

STOP

Language Arts

Skill Overview

A **complete sentence** has a subject and a verb and forms a complete thought.

A **sentence fragment** does not form a complete sentence.

Fragment	How to Correct	Corrected
Played soccer.	Add a subject.	*My friends and I played soccer.*
Our team.	Add a verb.	*Our team won the game.*

When writing a command, however, you do not need to include a subject. The subject *you* is understood. For example, the command *Pick up the garbage* is a complete sentence even though there is no *you*.

In a sentence that is written correctly, the subject and the verb agree. Both the subject and the verb are either singular or plural.

A **singular subject** names one person, place, thing, or idea. For example, *The girl eats an orange*. Both the subject (*girl*) and the verb (*eats*) are singular.

A **plural subject** names more than one person, place, thing, or idea. For example, *Maria, Thomas, and I do homework together. Maria, Thomas, and I* agree with the plural form of the verb *do*.

Punctuation helps readers understand sentences. **End punctuation** tells readers when to stop. End punctuation can also identify a sentence as a statement, a question, or an exclamation.

End Punctuation		
Period (.)	**Question Mark (?)**	**Exclamation Point (!)**
At the end of a statement.	At the end of a question.	To show strong feeling.
Today is Tuesday.	*What time is it?*	*I am so late!*

GO ON ▶

Skill Practice

1   **Which is the correct way to make this a complete sentence?**

> Most nights trouble falling asleep.

A   Most nights trouble was falling asleep.

B   Most nights Lauren's trouble falling asleep.

C   Most nights Lauren had trouble falling asleep.

D   Most nights falling asleep trouble.

2   **What is the correct punctuation mark for the end of the sentence?**

> Every night at bedtime, Rachel would whisper to her
> parents, "Can you stay awake until I fall asleep"

A   a period

B   a comma

C   a question mark

D   an exclamation point

3   **What is the correct way to write the underlined part of the sentence?**

> Yesterday, Mr. Takeo <u>show</u> us how to make a bird
> using the paper folding techniques of origami.

A   shows

B   showing

C   showed

D   showen

1 (A) (B) (C) (D)

2 (A) (B) (C) (D)

3 (A) (B) (C) (D)

4   **Which is the correct way to write the underlined word in the sentence?**

> The new game that we played <u>were</u> not much fun at all.

A   was

B   are

C   weren't

D   wasn't

5   **What is the BEST punctuation mark for the end of the sentence?**

> An hour later, it was clear that the dog was sound asleep

A   exclamation point

B   comma

C   semi colon

D   period

6   **Which is the correct way to write the underlined part of the sentence?**

> Could you please give me the orange crayon so I can
> use that <u>one, two</u>?

A   one, too

B   won, too

C   one, to

D   won, two

4 Ⓐ Ⓑ Ⓒ Ⓓ

5 Ⓐ Ⓑ Ⓒ Ⓓ

6 Ⓐ Ⓑ Ⓒ Ⓓ

GO ON ▶

7 **Which of these is a complete sentence?**

    A   Give me that phone.

    B   Tonight the full moon.

    C   Make sure you hold onto.

    D   The tallest pine tree, which also has the widest trunk.

8 **Which sentence uses the correct form of the verb?**

    A   Kerri and Jonathan does a great job on mural.

    B   Rocks and soil tumbles down the hill whenever it rains.

    C   The new bike really sparkle in the bright sunlight.

    D   A cheetah runs faster than a tiger.

9 **What is the BEST punctuation mark for the end of the sentence?**

> As the buzzer sounded, the crowd jumped up and
> yelled, "We won"

    A   a period

    B   a comma

    C   a question mark

    D   an exclamation point

7 Ⓐ Ⓑ Ⓒ Ⓓ
8 Ⓐ Ⓑ Ⓒ Ⓓ
9 Ⓐ Ⓑ Ⓒ Ⓓ

STOP ⬣

Writing to Narrate

Overview

Sometimes you will be asked to complete a **narrative** task. This means that you will write a story. You may be asked to write about something that you make up. You may be asked to write about something that actually happened. Sometimes you will be asked to write about only a part of a narrative, such as adding a beginning or an ending to a story. Your narrative writing should do the following:

Orient the Reader

Establish a situation. Make sure readers know what is happening and where it takes place. Introduce and describe the characters. You may want to use a narrator to tell the story. Be sure to organize your writing so that the reader can follow along as the events unfold.

Use Dialogue and Description

Use dialogue so that the reader knows what the different characters say to one another and how they respond to situations. Describe what the characters see and do and how they feel about what is happening.

Use Transitional Words and Phrases

Use transitional words to connect different parts of a story. Some transitional words show sequence, such as *In the beginning, first, second, then,* and *last.* These transitions will help your reader understand the order of events.

Use Concrete Words and Sensory Details

Use concrete words (*downpour* instead of *rain*, for example) and sensory details (words that appeal to the five senses: *plop, jagged,* and *crunchy,* for example) to help readers experience what you are describing.

Provide a Conclusion

Wrap up your writing with an ending or conclusion that makes sense based on what happens with the characters. If there is a problem that a character must solve, make sure you explain the solution in detail so your readers won't be confused about what happened.

GO ON ▶

Name _____ Date _____

Writing Practice

Read the text below. Then complete the task that follows.

The Day of the Penguins

Students were chattering and not paying attention to Mrs. Hass, their teacher. Suddenly the principal's voice boomed from the loudspeaker on the wall. "Good morning, children!"

All of the students quieted down so they could hear the morning announcements. As the principal talked, the classroom door creaked open. At first, there did not seem to be anyone there. Then Marty pointed. Sharese jumped up and shouted, "Look! Look!" The excitement spread as students gasped, giggled, and acted frightened and excited all at the same time.

At first, Mrs. Hass put her fingers to her lips to motion the students to be quiet. But when she turned around, she saw a penguin waddling into the classroom. Just behind that first penguin was another. Eventually, five penguins were waddling around the classroom, looking as curiously at the students as the students looked at them.

In the story, penguins waddle into a fourth-grade classroom. Think about how the students might respond and what questions they might have.

Write an ending for the story by adding details to tell what happens next. Use this space to help you plan your writing. Write your ending on a separate sheet of paper. Use your best cursive handwriting.

Planning

_____

_____

_____

STOP

Suffixes

Skill Overview

You might have read some unknown words in *Invasion from Mars*. Some of those words, such as *indescribable* and *rimless*, had suffixes that could help you figure out the meaning.

Figuring out the meaning of an unknown word calls for some "detective work." You can sometimes use context clues. Other clues can come from the word itself.

A **root word** is the main part of a word that gives the word its meaning. Some root words have word parts added to them. An **affix** is a word part added to a root word to change its meaning. A **suffix** is an affix added to the end of a word.

You can use the meanings of **suffixes** to figure out how they change the meanings of root words. Suffixes may sometimes change the part of speech of a word. For example, the suffixes *-ous* and *-y* change nouns into adjectives. Look at their meanings in the chart below.

Suffix	Meaning	Example
-ous	"full of"	joyous (full of joy)
-y	"in a state of"	misty

When you look at an unknown word, see if it has a suffix. Study the root word and the suffix. Think about how the suffix changes the meaning of the root word.

GO ON

Name _____ Date _____

Apply to Text

Read the passage below and answer the questions that follow.

An Enjoyable New Sport

> **Look Closely**
>
> Examine the word *cyclocross*.
> Look at the root word
> *-cross* and the prefix *cyclo-*
> separately to figure out the
> word's meaning.

1   Do you like to get out in the country? Do you feel comfortable on a bike? If so, when you grow up, you should try an event called cyclocross. In this demanding sport, you have to ride your bike and carry it!

2   You spend only part of the race on your bike because only half of the course is smooth. That half runs over pavement, smooth grass, and trails. The other half is harder. It goes though country fields, where bikers make their way over bumpy trails and up steep, woodsy hills. Bikers must even get over logs, sandpits, mud puddles, fences, and piles of wood. Several times during the race, riders must swiftly hop off their bikes. Then they hang their bikes over their shoulders and run as fast as their legs will carry them.

3   Determining when to ride and where to run is part of the strategy. At some points, hurdles force riders off their bikes. These hurdles are 10 to 15 inches high and are set close together. Racers must jump over the hurdles. As you can imagine, this is a perilous sport. There are dangers at every turn, so racers cannot be careless.

Name _____ Date _____

4   Races are fast and furious and last less than an hour from start to finish. A rider might be able to practice on an actual course to prepare for a race. Sometimes a rider can revisit a course to train.

5   Cyclocross bikes are like racing bikes, light in weight and with turned-down handlebars. Tires are narrow, but they have deep ruts in them that help the bikes get through dirt and mud.

6   Cyclocross began in Europe about fifteen years ago. The idea was to keep cyclists fit and healthy during the winter, as well as to help riders develop their skills and strength.

7   So, if you work out an hour a day, three or four days a week, you will probably be strong enough to compete. Don't get the wrong idea, though. The training is difficult, and the races themselves certainly can be dangerous. If you are strong, daring, and looking for adventure, then cyclocross might be just the thing for you.

1 What is the meaning of the word *bumpy*?

> It goes though country fields, where bikers make their way over <u>bumpy</u> trails and up steep, woodsy hills.

A   without bumps

B   not able to have bumps

C   in a state of having bumps

D   making large bumps on a soft surface

Look Closely

Think about how the suffix changes the meaning of the root word.

1 Ⓐ Ⓑ Ⓒ Ⓓ   **GO ON ▶**

Name _____ Date _____

2 **What is the meaning of the word *perilous*?**

> As you can imagine, this is a perilous sport.

A   full of peril

B   able to be in peril

C   the action of peril

D   one who is not in peril

3 **What is the meaning of the word *furious*?**

> Races are fast and furious and last less than an hour
> from start to finish.

A   without fury

B   filled with fury

C   an act of extreme fury

D   able to build fires quickly

Look Closely

What two word parts make up
the word *furious*? What do the
two parts mean?

4 **What is the meaning of the word *healthy*?**

> The idea was to keep cyclists fit and healthy during the
> winter, as well as to help riders develop their skills and
> strength.

A   without health

B   not completely safe

C   in a state of good health

D   to do something against good health

2 Ⓐ Ⓑ Ⓒ Ⓓ
3 Ⓐ Ⓑ Ⓒ Ⓓ
4 Ⓐ Ⓑ Ⓒ Ⓓ

STOP

Writing to Inform

Overview

Sometimes you will be asked to complete an **informative** task. This means writing about a topic or an idea. You may be asked to give information about a topic based on information that you have read. You may be asked to explain how to do something or how something works. Your informative texts should do the following:

Introduce the Topic and Organize Information

Introduce the topic and present information in a way that makes sense. Decide whether you will use illustrations or other visual elements. Consider whether section headings or numbers would help readers locate information or follow steps in a sequence. For example, some informative writing uses numbers to order the steps a person should follow.

Develop the Topic with Details and Examples

Organize and present details and examples compiled from your research. Include only those details and examples that clearly relate to your topic. Use facts, definitions, quotations, illustrations, and other visual elements to develop your topic.

Link Ideas

Use transitional words to connect sentences and paragraphs. Transitional words and phrases (*except, as well as, besides, if, first*, and *especially*, for example) link ideas in a meaningful way and help readers understand your writing.

Use Precise Language

Use precise language by selecting words with specific meanings that relate to the topic (*take all five beans* instead of *take the beans*, for example). Think about the terms and vocabulary you plan to use and consider whether you should define certain terms so readers will understand the points you are making.

Provide a Concluding Statement or Section

Wrap up your writing with a concluding statement or paragraph that restates your major point or points. Think about the most important idea you want to get across and create a summary or final sentence that readers will remember.

GO ON

Writing Practice

Read the informative text below. Then complete the task that follows.

	Player Two							Mancala Board
Player Two's Cup							Player One's Cup	
	Player One							

How to Play Mancala

Mancala is a game played in many different countries and with many different rules. In one basic game, two players take turns dropping beans into bins on a playing board. Players collect as many beans as possible until one player's bins are empty. The player with the most beans wins the game.

Game Setup You can play Mancala, too. You will need an egg carton without the lid, two cups, and 60 beans. The carton is your board. Place the board between the players. Place a cup to the right of each player's side of the board. Place five beans into each bin, or section of the carton. Then decide which player goes first.

Taking a Turn Choose one of the bins on your side of the board. Take all five beans out of the bin. Drop one bean into each of the bins to the right of the bin you emptied. After you drop a bean in the last bin on your side, put a bean into your cup at the end of the board. Continue to drop one bean into each of the bins on the other side of the board. If you still have beans when you reach the end of the other side, put one bean into the other player's cup.

Ending a Turn If the last bean dropped is in your cup, take another turn. If it is in an empty bin, take all the beans from the bin directly opposite and place them into your cup. Your turn is over. If you drop the last bean into a bin with other beans or into the other player's cup, your turn is over.

Ending the Game The game ends when all of the bins in front of one player are empty. The player who collects the most beans is the winner.

The text above explains one way to play Mancala. Think about a game or sport that you know well. Think about the equipment or materials needed to play and the rules for playing. Write an informative text that explains how to play the game you chose. Plan your writing and write your text on separate sheets of paper.

STOP

Name _____ Date _____

Figurative Language

How to Analyze the Text

In *Me and Uncle Romie,* the author uses phrases like "Uncle Romie's voice was like thunder" and "on top of the world." These phrases are examples of figurative language.

You will sometimes read phrases that you do not understand. You might know the meaning of each word, but the words together can be confusing. For example, you may know the words *get, cold,* and *feet,* but not the meaning of *get cold feet.*

> Before I go on stage, I get cold feet.

The phrase *get cold feet* is an example of figurative language. **Figurative language** uses vivid images or comparisons to create pictures in the reader's mind. Figurative language does not mean exactly what it says, so you have to figure it out. You can use nearby words as clues.

Idioms, similes, and metaphors are types of figurative language. An **idiom** is a familiar, commonly-used expression that does not have a word-for-word translation. You can use context clues to figure out the meaning.

> I love hiking and would do it at the drop of a hat.

Context clues show that the speaker loves to hike. The expression *at the drop of a hat* means "right away" or "at any time."

A **simile** uses the words *like* or *as* to compare ideas or things.

> Doug runs as fast as a cheetah.

A **metaphor** compares two things without using *like* or *as.*

> Life is a dream.

When you come across figurative language you do not understand, remember to use context clues to determine the meaning.

GO ON ▶

Name _____ Date _____

Apply to Text

Read the passage below and answer the questions that follow.

The After-School Club

1   Billy belonged to an after-school club. The purpose was to have fun while learning something new. Each week, a different member planned and ran the meeting. This week, it was Billy's turn. He was in the doghouse with the other members. The last time it was his turn, he cancelled the meeting, so he really needed to do something out of the ordinary to make it up to the group.

2   This week, he had everyone take a seat around the club's table. On the table was a large silk cloth covering objects. Billy snapped the cloth up from the table, like a magician performing a trick. All of the members looked with curiosity at the variety of items in front of them.

3   "You have only two minutes to memorize as many items as you can," Billy said. "It's a race against the clock." He produced a stopwatch from his pocket and, after yelling, "Go!" pushed the button. As the clock ticked, everyone concentrated on the objects. Their eyes were saucers, wide and unblinking. Then Billy announced that time was up and covered up the objects. He asked how many items each club member remembered.

4   "I remember scissors, a spoon, a sugar cube, and a strainer!" said Jan excitedly. "I memorized things that began with the same letter."

5   "I remember an apple, a cup, a glove, a rope, and a watch," Marco said. "I put things in alphabetical order."

6   "I remember the scissors and the knife, the thread and the rope, and the cup and the glass," said Ileana. "I tried to think of things that were similar in some way."

7   "I remember the glove, the rope, the apple, the strainer, and the scissors," said Rick, explaining that he used the first letters of some of the objects to make a word—GRASS.

Look Closely

Is Billy in an actual doghouse? Look at something that Billy has done that might give a clue to the meaning of the phrase.

Look Closely

Can children actually "race against a clock"? Look for word clues near the expression that will help explain its meaning. Think about what Billy has asked the other club members to do.

Name _____ Date _____

8   "Each of you had a different trick that helped you remember what you saw," said Billy. "I'll bet there are even more memory tricks that we should find out about!"

9   The members all agreed that Billy's club meeting was one of the best they'd ever had. They all had fun, and the meeting flew by in a flash. Billy was as proud as a peacock.

1   **What is the meaning of the idiom *in the doghouse* in Paragraph 1?**

> He was <u>in the doghouse</u> with the other members.

    A   in trouble

    B   ready to go

    C   not prepared

    D   popular with others

> **Look Closely**
>
> What did Billy do for his last meeting? How would the other members feel about him now? These answers help you figure out *in the doghouse*.

2   **Which describes the underlined expression?**

> Billy snapped the cloth up from the table, <u>like a magician performing a trick</u>.

    A   a simile that describes how Billy acts

    B   an idiom that describes how Billy feels

    C   a metaphor that describes how Billy acts

    D   a simile that describes what a magic trick looks like

1 Ⓐ Ⓑ Ⓒ Ⓓ
2 Ⓐ Ⓑ Ⓒ Ⓓ

GO ON ▶

Name _____ Date _____

3 **What does the metaphor *their eyes were saucers* mean in Paragraph 3?**

> Their eyes were saucers, wide and unblinking.

A   Their eyes were hard and cold.

B   Their eyes were almost closed shut.

C   Their eyes were opened wide and round.

D   Their eyes showed that they were very hungry.

> **Look Closely**
>
> Think about what saucers would look like in place of someone's eyes to figure out the meaning of the metaphor.

4 **What does it mean to *race against the clock*?**

> "It's a race against the clock."

A   The clocks are running fast.

B   There can be only one winner.

C   It is time to stop doing the activity.

D   There is little time to finish the task.

5 **What does the expression *in a flash* mean?**

> They all had fun, and the meeting flew by in a flash.

A   completely

B   quickly

C   quietly

D   smoothly

> **Look Closely**
>
> The club members are having fun. How does time go by for you when you are having fun?

6 **What does the simile mean?**

> Billy was as proud as a peacock.

A   Billy acted like a bird.

B   Billy looked like a peacock.

C   Billy thought peacocks were fancy.

D   Billy felt like a pleased, strutting peacock.

3   Ⓐ Ⓑ Ⓒ Ⓓ
4   Ⓐ Ⓑ Ⓒ Ⓓ
5   Ⓐ Ⓑ Ⓒ Ⓓ
6   Ⓐ Ⓑ Ⓒ Ⓓ

STOP

Writing and Research

Overview

Sometimes you will be asked to write an analysis of two or more pieces of writing. Sometimes digital and multimedia sources will be included. You may be asked to compare and contrast the selections. In this case, you would write about how the two sources are similar and how they are different. In all cases, you will be asked to use evidence from the texts to support your analysis and reflection.

Orient the Reader

Let the reader know what you are writing about. Write a beginning paragraph that clearly introduces your topic.

Create an Organizational Structure

Organize your essay so that related ideas are grouped to support your purpose.

• You might organize your essay by points: State a point and give an example from each text.

• You might organize your essay by topics: State several points and give examples from one text before moving on to the next text and addressing the same points.

Cite Evidence

Use examples from each text to support the ideas in your writing. For example, if you agree with one writer and disagree with the other, give examples and explain why.

Use Transitional Words and Phrases

Use a variety of transitional words and phrases to link ideas in your writing. Examples include *for example, in order to, in addition, because,* and *also.*

Use Precise Language

Use words that tell exactly what you mean. Also, use vocabulary that is specific to the topic. If you are not sure the reader will know a vocabulary word, define it.

Provide a Conclusion

Wrap up your writing with a concluding statement or paragraph. A conclusion should summarize the main points of the writing. You might also refer back to something important stated in the beginning of your writing.

GO ON

Writing Practice

Read the two texts that follow. Take notes on each one. After you read, follow the directions to write an essay about what you have read.

Cumberland Island National Seashore

Cumberland Island lies off the Atlantic coast of Georgia. The island is preserved as a national seashore. No bridge connects the island to the mainland. The only way to get there is by boat. You can catch a ferry at St. Mary's on the mainland.

Cumberland Island National Seashore is a great place to hike, bike, camp, and more. Fifty miles of hiking trails take you through forests and marshes. You'll go past beaches and historic places. You can walk or rent a bicycle. Camping is allowed. Some campgrounds have showers and bathrooms. Other campgrounds have no facilities and campers must treat the water before they drink it. Other outdoor activities include hunting and fishing.

The area is home to all kinds of wildlife. Birdwatchers especially will enjoy the more than 335 kinds of birds that live on the island or stop over while migrating to other places. Other wildlife includes manatees, sea turtles, dolphins, wild turkeys, and lizards.

The island has several important historic structures, including the ruins of a mansion built in 1884. Another historic building is the First African Baptist Church. It was built in the 1890s for the African American workers on the island.

Cumberland Island National Seashore is a beautiful place. It is meant to be enjoyed by people today and preserved for future generations to enjoy.

What might you enjoy most while visiting Cumberland Island National Seashore?

_____

_____

_____

_____

National Park Service

Cumberland Island National Seashore is just one of the many places managed by the National Park Service (NPS). This federal agency is responsible for preserving and maintaining nearly 400 national parks, seashores, monuments, historic sites, and other special places.

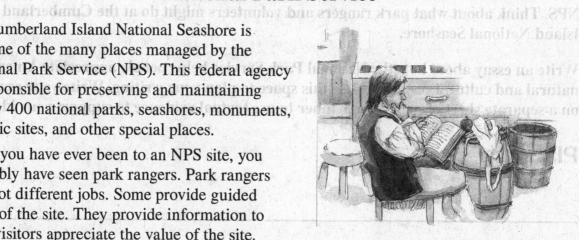

If you have ever been to an NPS site, you probably have seen park rangers. Park rangers do a lot different jobs. Some provide guided tours of the site. They provide information to help visitors appreciate the value of the site. Some rangers are law enforcement officers. They keep peace and make sure no one is breaking laws. Some rangers also handle medical emergencies, firefighting, and search and rescue operations.

Taking care of all the NPS sites is a big job. Rangers get help from volunteers. Some volunteers answer questions about the history of a park. They might give directions about where to find specific things at the park. At historic sites volunteers might dress in the clothing of that time period. They talk to visitors "in character" to show what it would have been like to live in the area at that time.

One goal of the National Park Service is to protect our nation's natural and cultural resources. Then people can enjoy them for generations to come. The park rangers and volunteers cannot do this alone. Here is a saying that helps explain how they want visitors to behave when they come: "Leave nothing behind but footprints. Take nothing but pictures."

Would you like to be a volunteer for the National Park Service? Why or why not?

_____

_____

_____

_____

GO ON ▶

You have read two texts about the National Park Service and one of the sites of the NPS. Think about what park rangers and volunteers might do at the Cumberland Island National Seashore.

Write an essay about how the National Park Service helps people appreciate America's natural and cultural resources. Use this space to plan your writing. Write your essay on a separate sheet of paper. Remember to use textual evidence to support your ideas.

Planning

_____

_____

_____

_____

_____

_____

_____

_____

_____

_____

_____

_____

_____

STOP

Name _____ Date _____

Poetry

How to Analyze the Text

Poems often use the way words sound to show meaning. Some poems have a rhythm that you can count out in beats. Some poems use rhyming words. Some poems use onomatopoeia to help you "hear" the sounds the writer is describing. The chart below shows some of the tools writers use in their poems.

rhyme	lines that end the same way *Broken gravel covers the street.* *It really is rough on your feet!*
alliteration	words that start with the same sound *Sarah sells socks on State Street.* *Tammy tells tales to Tanya.*
simile	comparisons using *like* or *as* *The leather felt as smooth as butter.* *Dad was angry and roared like a lion.*
metaphor	comparisons *Julie's home run was a real rocket.*
antonyms	opposites *The sand was not rough; it was soft and smooth fabric across the shore.*
onomatopoeia	words that say their own sound *buzz, beep*
repetition	lines, phrases, or ideas that are repeated in a poem

GO ON ▶

Name _____ Date _____

Apply to Text

Read the poem below and answer the questions that follow.

Waiting for Dinner

1   A tiger and bear
    Were lying in a cave.
    The tiger began growling,
    And the bear said, "You behave."

5   The tiger whined, "I'm hungry,
    I've had nothing to eat for hours,"
    The bear said, "Stop your grumbling
    And take time to smell the flowers."

    The angry tiger bellowed,
10 "Flowers won't fill my tummy!"
    And the bear replied calmly,
    "But their scent is just like honey."

    The tiger leaped out of the cave,
    In search of something tasty.
15 He ran right into a super swarm
    Of angry honeybees.

    The bear smelled all the flowers
    That surrounded his hollow home
    Then quietly followed the buzzing bees
20 Back to their honeycomb.

    As he licked the dripping honey
    Off his paws and ate for hours
    The bear said, "I told the tiger
    To take time to smell the flowers."

Look Closely
Examine the structure of the lines on the page.

1 How can you tell that "Waiting for Dinner" is a poem? Give TWO details about its structure to support your answer.

_____

_____

_____

_____

_____

2 Which line or lines from the poem include examples of alliteration? How do you know? Use evidence from the poem to support your answer.

_____

_____

_____

_____

_____

GO ON ▶

3 Find TWO pairs of rhyming words in the poem. How do you know they rhyme? Use evidence from the poem to support your answer.

_____

_____

_____

_____

4 What is an example of repetition in the poem? How is it used? Use evidence from the poem to support your answer.

_____

_____

_____

_____

Name _____ Date _____

Language Arts

Skill Overview

A noun names a person, place, or thing. A proper noun names a specific person, place, thing, or idea. When writing, use a capital letter to signal that a word is a proper noun.

Proper Nouns	
People or Groups	Richard James, Girl Scouts, Americans
Personal Titles	Aunt Debbie, Dr. Carter, Mr. Edwards
Places	Grand Canyon, Warwick Street

Apostrophes can be used to identify possessive nouns, or ownership. *The teacher used Mary's pen to grade the students' papers.*

A pronoun can take the place of a noun in a sentence.

Pronoun Rule	Example
A pronoun must agree with the noun it replaces.	Incorrect: *The dog found the bone and ate <u>them</u>.* Correct: *The dog found the bone and ate <u>it</u>.*
Use the correct case, or form, of a pronoun.	Incorrect: *The students opened they books.* Correct: *The students opened <u>their</u> books.*

In a sentence that is written correctly, the subject and the verb agree. Both the subject and the verb are either singular or plural.

Avoid using double negatives when you write. A **double negative** happens when two negative words are used in one sentence. Negative words include *no, not, never, none, nothing,* and *nobody.* Incorrect: *They do not like no loud noises.* Correct: *They do not like loud noises.*

Be careful to spell words correctly and remember to use spelling patterns you know.

GO ON ▶

Name _____ Date _____

Skill Practice

1 **What is the correct way to write the underlined part of the sentence?**

> My aunt has a cabin on a lake near augusta, georgia.

A   Augusta, georgia

B   augusta, Georgia

C   Augusta, Georgia

D   Augusta of Georgia

2 **Which is the correct way to write the underlined word?**

> When I went to visit him, I got to rid his horse.

A   read

B   rode

C   ride

D   riding

3 **What is the correct way to write the sentence?**

> At first, I did not want to go to no circus.

A   At first, I did not want to go to a circus.

B   At first, I want to go no circus.

C   At first, I did not go to no circus.

D   In the first place, I did not want to go to no circus.

1 Ⓐ Ⓑ Ⓒ Ⓓ
2 Ⓐ Ⓑ Ⓒ Ⓓ
3 Ⓐ Ⓑ Ⓒ Ⓓ

4 **Which is the correct way to write the underlined part of the sentence?**

My uncle put him arm on my shoulder to comfort me.

A put he's arm

B put his arm

C put my arm

D put him's arm

5 **Which word correctly completes the sentence?**

The carriage driver held the _____ and did not let go.

A reigns

B raynes

C reins

D rains

6 **Which is the correct way to write the underlined part of the sentence?**

Alex wanted to borrow the pen that belonged to Dominic.

A Dominic's pen

B Dominic pen

C Dominic pen's

D Dominics pen

4 Ⓐ Ⓑ Ⓒ Ⓓ
5 Ⓐ Ⓑ Ⓒ Ⓓ
6 Ⓐ Ⓑ Ⓒ Ⓓ

GO ON

Name _____ Date _____

7   **Which word correctly completes the sentence?**

> The computer screens all went blank and no one was able
> to read _____.

A   it

B   those

C   these

D   them

8   **Which is the correct way to write the underlined part of the sentence?**

> On Fridays, Maria <u>take</u> out the trash.

A   takes

B   taking

C   took

D   taken

9   **Which is the correct way to write the underlined part of the sentence?**

> Mr. Murphy said we would need to raise <u>alot</u> of money
> for our class trip .

A   allot

B   lot

C   a lots

D   a lot

Synonyms and Antonyms

Skill Overview

The selection *The Earth Dragon Awakes* includes word pairs such as *shout* and *holler*, in which the words have roughly the same meaning. It also includes word pairs such as *creep* and *bolt*, in which the words have opposite meanings.

Words that have the same or similar meanings are called **synonyms**. In the sentence below, the words *stop* and *cease* are synonyms.

> When the coach tells us to stop, we cease running right away.

Words that have opposite meanings are known as **antonyms**. In the sentence below, the words *entertaining* and *dull* are antonyms.

> I thought the movie was entertaining, but my sister thought it was very dull.

Synonyms and antonyms can help you figure out unknown words. Look for words such as *but*. In the sentence about the movie, the word *but* tells you that the speaker and the sister hold very different opinions about the movie. If you knew what *dull* meant, you could use that information to find out the meaning of *entertaining*: *entertaining* would mean more or less the opposite of *dull*.

Synonyms and antonyms can also help you solve analogies. An **analogy** compares two pairs of words that have the same relationship.

> wet : dry :: hot : cold

You can read this as "*wet* is related to *dry* in the same way that *hot* is related to *cold*." Check that this is true: *wet* and *dry* are antonyms, and *hot* and *cold* are antonyms, too. The relationship connects the words in each pair in the same way.

In an analogy problem, the last word is often missing. Your job is to find it by thinking about the relationship between the first pair of words, and then by applying that relationship to the second pair of words. Here is an example:

> smart : intelligent :: difficult : _____

Smart and *intelligent* are synonyms. The words in the other pair must be synonyms too. So, the missing word must mean roughly the same as *difficult* such as *hard*, *tough*, or *rugged*.

GO ON ▶

Name _____ Date _____

Apply to Text

Read the passage below and answer the questions that follow.

John Ringling

1   John Ringling was a businessman, a circus owner, an art collector, and more. He was born on May 31, 1866, in Iowa. As a young man, Ringling decided to start a circus with his brothers. Their plan was to travel from one town to another, performing as they went. Although John Ringling appeared in the show at first, he soon became bored with performing and realized he was more interested in helping to run the business. Soon he took on the job of deciding what towns the circus would visit and in what order. Ringling traveled to those towns ahead of the circus to tell people about it and make them eager to see the show in person.

2   John Ringling also made some important changes in the way the brothers' circus operated. In 1890, for instance, he convinced his brothers that the circus should travel by train. Before that, every member of the circus—and every piece of equipment as well—traveled in wagons pulled by horses. Soon the Ringling Brothers Circus had its own train, which included almost 100 cars. It took that many to transport all the people, animals, and gear the circus required. Compared to the slow and exhausting wagon travel that the Ringlings had used earlier, train travel was swift and easy.

3   In 1907, Ringling and his brothers purchased the Barnum and Bailey Circus. Though the Barnum and Bailey Circus had been both large and very well-known, it was beginning to lose money, and its owners were happy to sell out to the Ringlings. The expansion made the Ringling Brothers' circus one of the largest in the country. Once, John Ringling and his brothers had been obscure circus performers. Now, the Ringling Brothers were famous everywhere they went.

Look Closely

Synonyms are words that have nearly the same meaning. What is a synonym for *business* in this paragraph?

Look Closely

Look for clue words and phrases like *although, but,* and *compared to.* They often signal that a pair of words are antonyms.

Look Closely

Antonyms have opposite meanings. Look for words that tell how things are different.

4   Profits from the circus soon made John Ringling quite wealthy. He began investing his money in other businesses, including oil companies and railroads. Ringling became especially interested in buying land in towns and cities along the Gulf Coast. He built houses and hotels on his new land, hoping to turn municipalities into vacation destinations.

5   Besides circuses and real estate, Ringling was also deeply interested in art. He spent much of his wealth on famous paintings and sculptures. Toward the end of the 1920s, Ringling used his fortune to build a museum near his home so he could display his artworks. The museum was built in part with the assistance of elephants from Ringling's own circus; they provided help in putting the stones where they belonged. Though Ringling died in 1936 at the age of 70, the museum remains open to visitors.

1   **Which word from the passage BEST completes the analogy?**

worried : anxious :: enthusiastic : _____

A   bored

B   eager

C   famous

D   quite

1 Ⓐ Ⓑ Ⓒ Ⓓ   GO ON ▶

2 **Which word has the opposite meaning of the word *slow*?**

> Compared to the <u>slow</u> and exhausting wagon travel that
> the Ringlings had used earlier, train travel was swift
> and easy.

A easy

B exhausting

C sluggish

D swift

Look Closely

Look at the phrase at the
beginning of the sentence.
What does that phrase often
tell you about how word pairs
are related?

3 **Which words from the passage are opposite
in meaning?**

A money, profits

B obscure, famous

C purchased, interested

D expansion, largest

4 **Which word has almost the SAME meaning as the
word *wealth*?**

> He spent much of his <u>wealth</u> on famous paintings
> and sculptures.

A assistance

B travel

C fortune

D instance

2 Ⓐ Ⓑ Ⓒ Ⓓ
3 Ⓐ Ⓑ Ⓒ Ⓓ
4 Ⓐ Ⓑ Ⓒ Ⓓ

STOP

Name _____ Date _____

Writing Opinions

Overview

Sometimes you will be asked to write an **opinion**. This means writing to tell what you think about a topic and giving the reasons for why you think as you do. You might be asked to write your opinion about an idea, an event, or a person. Your written opinion should do the following:

Introduce a Topic

Write a clear beginning paragraph that introduces your topic. Near the end of the paragraph, state your opinion on the topic. If you are writing an opinion about a text, state the title of the text.

Create an Organizational Structure

Organize your writing in a way that makes sense. For example, if you want to present three supporting reasons for your opinion, you might write a separate paragraph for each of those reasons.

Provide Reasons

Provide reasons for your opinion and support the reasons with facts and examples. If you are writing an opinion about a text, use details and examples taken directly from the passage. If you are writing an opinion about an idea, person, or event, you might use details and examples from reference materials or from your own experiences.

Link Reasons to the Opinion

Use transitional words to connect your opinion with the reasons you provide. You can use transitional words such as *because, however, for example*, and *for this reason* to show how your reasons support your opinion.

Provide a Conclusion

Wrap up your writing with a concluding statement or paragraph. The conclusion should restate your opinion and might summarize your reasons. Most important, your conclusion should leave readers with a clear understanding of your opinion.

GO ON

Writing Practice

Read the text below. Then complete the task that follows.

A Simple Nutrition Guide

The evidence is in. Most Americans have some very unhealthy eating habits. We often eat too much food and too many fatty and sweet foods. But how can you decide if you are eating healthy meals? Just look at your plate—MyPlate, that is. MyPlate is a nutrition guide from the United States Department of Agriculture. It makes planning healthy meals simple and fun.

The MyPlate diagram shows that half of the foods we eat should be fruits and vegetables. The other half should be grains and proteins. Quality and quantity of these foods also matter. Whole grains are better than refined grains. Fresh fruits and vegetables are better than canned. Fish, poultry, and beans are healthier protein choices than red meat. Most dairy choices should be fat-free or low-fat products. Portion sizes should be on the smaller side. Also, avoid second helpings.

MyPlate does not include foods with added sugar such as cakes and cookies. It also does not include foods with a lot of solid fats such as ice cream and hot dogs. These kinds of foods contain few or no nutrients that keep our bodies healthy. Most people eat too many of these "empty calories."

MyPlate is a useful tool for healthy eating. If you balance the kinds of foods you eat and cut down on the amount of empty calories, you'll be doing your body a big favor.

The text above discusses ways to make healthy food choices. Think about the nutrition of the lunches you eat at school.

Do your school lunches provide good nutrition? Write an essay that gives your opinion about this topic. Use this space to help you plan your writing. Write your essay on a separate sheet of paper. Cite evidence from the text above to support your ideas.

Planning

_____

_____

STOP

Name _____ Date _____

Text and Graphic Features

How to Analyze the Text

The Life and Times of the Ant includes text and graphic features. The text features include headings and captions. Some of the graphic features are a timeline, a chart, and illustrations.

Text features are special types of text that help the reader find information. Headings, for example, tell what each section of a text is about.

Graphic features show information in a visual way. They include outlines, timelines, graphic organizers, charts, diagrams, maps, photos, and illustrations.

An outline organizes the main points of a text with a title, headings, and subheadings. For example:

Benefits of a Vegetable Garden

I. Exercise

II. Food
   A. cheaper
   B. healthier
      1. more vitamins
      2. fresher

III. Environment
   A. organic
   B. local
   C. less waste

A timeline organizes events in the order they happened. For example:

A graphic organizer shows how facts or ideas relate to each other. Examples include T-charts, story maps, and Venn diagrams.

GO ON ▶

Name _____ Date _____

Apply to Text

Read the passage below and answer the questions that follow.

My Adventures as an Explorer

1   My name is Alvar Nuñez Cabeza de Vaca. I was born in Spain in 1490. My parents were Spanish nobles. The family name *Cabeza de Vaca* means "head of a cow."

Disaster in Florida

2   On June 17, 1527, I became an explorer, joining captain Panfilo de Narváez and a crew of 300 men sailing west. First, we went to Hispaniola, and then we sailed to Cuba, where we had some excitement—a hurricane. Storms blew our ships to a place now called "Florida." On April 12, 1528, we landed near Tampa Bay and claimed it for Spain.

3   We docked the boat and explored the land, but things quickly started going wrong. There were more hurricanes, and we fought with the natives. Food and water were scarce. Our pilot, who had stayed behind with the ship, got scared and sailed off to Mexico without us. When we returned to the ship, it was gone!

Shipwrecked

4   We wanted to get to Mexico to find the Spanish settlements, so we built five rough boats and headed off. We hit more bad weather, lost three of the boats and many of the men, and were running out of supplies. On November 6, 1528, our two remaining boats shipwrecked on Galveston Island. It turns out that we were the first Europeans to set foot on land that would later become Texas.

5   We suffered through a cold winter with the help of the Karankawa Indians. The 15 men who survived then started walking along the Colorado River, looking for food and trading with natives. For several years, we struggled for survival. By 1533, another eleven men had died.

> **Look Closely**
>
> Before reading, look at the headings to find out what each section of the passage is about.

> **Look Closely**
>
> Note the dates throughout the passage. They can help you create a timeline or answer questions about one.

Interesting Adventures

6   There were, however, some interesting adventures, too. For example, we were the first Europeans to see the amazing American buffalo. Some natives thought I was a medicine man, so I performed the first known surgical operation in Texas. Using a flint knife, I removed an arrowhead from a Karankawa Indian.

7   We kept walking and walking. Our trek included a walk to Mexico City, where we met the famous *conquistador* Hernán Cortés, who had conquered much of Mexico. In April 1537, I returned to Spain.

My Return to Spain

8   Back in Spain, I wrote about my adventures and about the mistreatment of natives by the Spanish conquerors. My ideas were published as *La Relacion* ("The Journal") in 1542. In 1541, I was appointed as a governor in South America. My lenient laws, however, were unpopular in Spain. So, I was recalled by the King, convicted, and then pardoned. I lived the rest of my life as a judge in Seville, Spain. I died there in 1557.

1   **Based on the passage, which event belongs in the empty box in the timeline?**

1490 — Cabeza de Vaca born
1527 — leaves Spain on an expedition
1528 —
1537 — returns to Spain

A   explores Florida and Texas

B   publishes *La Relacion*

C   becomes a governor

D   moves to Seville

Look Closely

Examine the text for events that happened in the year 1528.

1 (A) (B) (C) (D)   GO ON ▶

2 **Which section of the passage gives details about Cabeza's landing in Tampa Bay?**

   A   Interesting Adventures

   B   My Return to Spain

   C   Disaster in Florida

   D   Shipwrecked

Look Closely

Look for details in the passage about Cabeza in Tampa Bay and note the section heading.

3 **Which event did NOT happen in Texas?**

   A   Cabeza met Cortés.

   B   Cabeza saw buffalo.

   C   Cabeza performed an operation.

   D   Cabeza shipwrecked on Galveston Island.

Look Closely

Look for the events listed in the answer choices. Which one did NOT happen in Texas?

4 **What is the main idea of the picture?**

   A   The boy and his father enjoy getting a boat ready.

   B   The people in the photo do not like boating.

   C   The boy is great at sailing.

   D   A terrible storm is coming.

2 Ⓐ Ⓑ Ⓒ Ⓓ

3 Ⓐ Ⓑ Ⓒ Ⓓ

4 Ⓐ Ⓑ Ⓒ Ⓓ

STOP

Main Idea and Details

How to Analyze the Text

Ecology for Kids is mostly about the delicate balance between the environment and the organisms that live there. That message is the main idea of the passage.

Every passage you read has a main idea. The **main idea** tells what the passage is mostly about.

You can look for main ideas in paragraphs, too. Each paragraph in a nonfiction passage has a main idea. The main idea of each paragraph helps tell about the main idea of the whole passage.

Sometimes it is easy to find a main idea, because the main idea is clearly stated. Other times, you need to work harder to find out what a passage or paragraph is mostly about. Supporting **details** are clues that tell about the main idea.

Details can:

- answer questions such as who, what, where, when, why, and how

- explain a main idea

- give facts, reasons, or examples that support a main idea

Here is an example:

Main Idea: Georgia contains many different landforms.

- In the north, the Blue Ridge Mountains include the highest point in the state, Brasstown Bald.

- Sand hills stretch across the state from Augusta to Columbus.

- The Okefenokee Swamp lies at Georgia's southeast border with Florida.

Name _____ Date _____

How to Analyze the Text

Read the passage below and answer the questions that follow.

In a Tizzy for Tulips

	Look Closely
	Read and think about the title. It often gives a hint to what the passage is mostly about.

1   Can you imagine a flower that costs as much as a house? In the 1600s, someone paid that much for a red and white tulip called the *Semper Augustus*. It was the most expensive tulip in history.

2   Tulips first came from Turkey. The word *tulip* comes from a Turkish word that means "turban." The bell-shaped flowers look a little like turbans. Turbans are wraps that men in some parts of the world wear on their heads.

Look Closely

Notice that the word *turban* repeats in the paragraph. That gives you a clue that the most important idea in this paragraph is that tulips look like turbans.

3   In the 1500s, the tulip was brought to Europe. Over the years, it became a fashionable flower. That was especially true in the Netherlands. Beginning in 1634, collecting and planting tulips became such a craze there that it was given a name: *tulipomania*. People spent huge amounts of money on tulip bulbs. One man gave a tulip dealer a suit, a bed, 24 farm animals, and much more for just one tulip bulb.

Look Closely

Identify and make a list of the main idea of each paragraph. This can help you figure out the main idea of the entire passage.

4   No one knows why tulips became so wildly popular in the Netherlands. Maybe it was because they were so different from other flowers in that part of the world. In fact, when tulip bulbs first arrived in Europe, few people knew what they were. One merchant thought they looked like onions, so he roasted them and ate them! But once Europeans realized that the bulbs produced beautiful flowers when they were planted, they were eager to get as many tulips as they could. At first they imported the plants from Turkey, but soon they began growing bulbs

in the Netherlands and selling them to customers there
and in nearby countries. Tulipomania was beginning.

5   Some people in the Netherlands bought tulips simply
because the flowers were pretty and they wanted to make
their gardens beautiful. But other people had different
reasons for buying the plants. Many wanted to impress
their friends and relatives by showing them what good
taste they had. And quite a few hoped to make money by
buying and selling tulips. They expected that the price of
tulips would rise steadily. Then they could sell the tulips
again for more money than they had originally spent.
For a while this was true, as prices climbed to enormous
levels. But, in 1637, people began to realize that the
prices were too high. They stopped overpaying for tulips.
That marked the end of tulipomania.

6   Still, tulips remain extremely popular in the
Netherlands. Indeed, tulip production is a major industry
in the Netherlands today. About three billion bulbs are
produced there every year. Almost half of the country's
land is planted with tulips! Along with wooden clogs and
windmills, the tulip is considered an important symbol
of the Netherlands.

1   **What is the main idea of Paragraph 3? Use evidence from the text to support
your answer.**

_____

_____

_____

_____

_____

GO ON ▶

2 Why were people willing to pay such large sums for tulips? Give TWO details
from the passage to support your answer.

_____

_____

_____

_____

3 Think about how the author organized the information in the passage.
Complete the graphic organizer with the main idea from the passage.

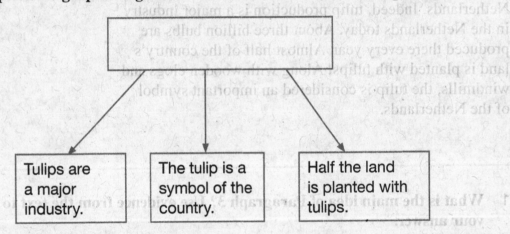

Explain how the three details support the main idea. Use text evidence to
support your answer.

_____

_____

_____

_____

STOP

Speech

How to Analyze the Text

Giving a Speech

Giving a speech is a good way to share what you have learned, to honor a special person, or to convince people to help out with a project.

Before you write a speech, you may need to find information in books and magazines, or on the Internet, to support your ideas.

- Encyclopedias and books can give you basic facts about a topic.

- If you need the most up-to-date facts about a topic or issue, magazines and Web sites offer current information.

- Be careful to choose Web sites you can trust. For example, Web sites sponsored by the U.S. government or your state government offer reliable facts about many science and history topics.

When you give a speech, think about your purpose and audience. Speak carefully so that everyone can hear and understand your ideas. It's a good idea to include pictures, videos, or sound effects to help explain your topic and to make your speech interesting.

Listening to a Speech

Good listeners look at the speaker and pay attention. They are careful to sit quietly and not interrupt. Listen carefully for the main idea of the speech. Most speakers will explain their main point at the beginning of their speech. Once you understand the main idea, listen carefully for details that support the idea. When the speech is over, you can summarize the ideas and then ask the speaker to clarify any points you did not understand.

GO ON

Name _____ Date _____

Apply to Text

Read the passage below and answer the questions that follow.

Save the Bats!

1   Most people are afraid
of bats and think of them as
creepy blood-suckers. But
bats are really our friends
and help us in many ways.
That's why we need to save
the bats and protect the
places where they live.

2   One way that bats help
us is by eating mosquitoes. A single bat can eat over
a thousand mosquitoes in just one hour! Bats also eat
insects that damage farmers' crops. If there are enough
bats around, then farmers don't need to use as many
chemicals on their crops to kill insects.

3   Some bats even pollinate the flowers of fruit trees.
That means they spread the pollen from the trees'
flowers, so the trees can make fruits. Bats also help
spread the seeds of plants so that more of them will grow
in new places.

4   Today, some kinds of bats are in danger of dying out.
That's because we are harming their habitats, the places
where they live and find food. There are two kinds of
bats on Georgia's endangered species list. These are the
gray bat and the Indiana bat. Scientists are studying them
so they can find ways to help save the bats.

5   You can help keep bats alive, too. Stay out of caves
where there are signs showing they are bat habitats.
Don't harm bats in your neighborhood, but if you find
a bat, leave it alone. Like other wild animals, bats will
bite you in self-defense if you bother them, and they can
spread diseases.

> **Look Closely**
>
> Read closely and think about
> the title and Paragraph 1 of
> the speech. What is the main
> idea Jacob wants you to know
> about bats?

> **Look Closely**
>
> What details in Paragraphs 2
> and 3 support Jacob's main
> idea about bats?

Name _____ Date _____

1 What is the speech MAINLY about?

A   why bats are dangerous

B   how bats pollinate flowers

C   why we need to protect bats

D   how to locate a bat cave

2 If you were in the audience when Jacob was giving his speech, what would be the MOST polite thing you could do?

A   show interest by asking questions about bats

B   help Jacob by explaining what hibernation is

C   make a list of your favorite movies about bats

D   listen carefully to Jacob and not interrupt

3 What is the BEST summary of Jacob's speech?

A   We need to beware of bats because they carry dangerous germs and are a threat to other animals.

B   We need to save bats because they eat harmful insects, pollinate flowers, and spread seeds.

C   Georgia has more endangered bats than any other state, so it is up to us to protect them.

D   Some bats are harmful, some are harmless, and others actually help us.

1 Ⓐ Ⓑ Ⓒ Ⓓ

2 Ⓐ Ⓑ Ⓒ Ⓓ

3 Ⓐ Ⓑ Ⓒ Ⓓ

GO ON ▶

4 Which of these would be BEST for Jacob to share with the audience at the end of his speech?

A a video showing bats pollinating flowers

B an audio recording of the sounds bats make

C a chart showing all Georgia endangered animals

D directions to the Georgia Department of Natural Resources

5 Which of these would be the BEST source for learning more about endangered bats in Georgia?

A a nonfiction book titled *Amazing Creatures*

B an online encyclopedia article about endangered animals

C a magazine article called "Build Your Own Bat House"

D a government Web site about Georgia wildlife

4 Ⓐ Ⓑ Ⓒ Ⓓ
5 Ⓐ Ⓑ Ⓒ Ⓓ

STOP

Sequence of Events

How to Analyze the Text

In *The Right Dog for the Job*, the puppy Ira goes through a series of steps to become a service dog. First, Ira lives with a foster puppy raiser and learns basic skills. Next, he goes to service-dog training. Last, he graduates and goes to live with Don.

When authors tell a story, they usually start at the beginning and follow the steps through to the end. Telling events in the order they happen is one way that authors can connect ideas. This pattern is called **chronological order**.

As you read, look for words and phrases that the author uses to organize the **sequence of events**. These clues include *after, before, earlier, finally, first, just as, while, next, until,* and *yesterday*. Dates and times, such as *1971, April 13,* or *10:30 A.M.*, also help put events in order.

In this example, the story events are told in chronological order. Pay attention to clue words that help you follow the order of events. Then look at how the chart below summarizes the sequence.

> The Changs had a lot to do. First, they cleaned the house. They swept, dusted, and put things away. Next they set up tables and chairs in the yard. After that, they made burgers for the cookout. Finally, everything was ready for their guests.

They cleaned the house. → They set up tables and chairs. → They made the burgers.

GO ON ▶

Name _____ Date _____

Apply to Text

Read the passage below and answer the questions that follow.

The Art Experiment

1   The yellow fliers announced that the school art contest had arrived. For years, Stan and Jill had won a prize by painting a colorful animal. This year, Jill surprised Stan by saying, "I'm tired of doing the same old thing every year. I've been learning about all different kinds of art in class. I think we should do something different."

2   Stan liked winning prizes. He had to admit, though, that it would be fun to try something new. He figured there was plenty of time to make an animal painting if the other projects didn't work out, so he agreed to Jill's idea.

3   The next weekend, their neighbor Mrs. Franco taught Stan and Jill pottery in her basement studio. First, they kneaded clay to make it soft. Next, they rolled the clay into slabs and coils. Stan and Jill made the pieces into a sculpture. Then Mrs. Franco baked the sculpture in a hot oven called a kiln. After it cooled, they painted it with special paints called glazes. The sculpture baked in the kiln again, and the glazes formed into a hard surface. The finished piece looked like a tall tree blowing in the wind.

> **Look Closely**
>
> Look for the time order words in Paragraph 3 to help you figure out the order of events.

4   A week later, Stan and Jill tried papier-mâché. They mixed flour and hot water. While the paste cooled, they built a cardboard armature, or frame, by taping paper towel rolls and cardboard box pieces into the shape of a pig. Then they dipped strips of newspaper in the flour paste and wrapped them around the frame. When the sticky paper dried and turned hard, Stan and Jill painted the pig hot pink. It looked a little crooked, but very cheerful.

> **Look Closely**
>
> Note that the steps for making papier-mâché are in order. Retell the steps in your own words to remember the sequence of events.

5   Finally, Stan and Jill built a model plane with popsicle sticks, macaroni, and toothpicks. They sketched a plan and then started gluing the pieces together. Once the glue dried, they painted the plane and signed their names in tiny letters, one on each wing.

> **Look Closely**
>
> Look for a clue word that tells you that model building is the last project.

Name _____ Date _____

6   With all three projects finished, Jill asked Stan what
he thought. Stan reported that he had a great time with
each new project. "I might never paint another animal
again," he said. "But which project will we enter in the
art contest?"

7   Jill laughed and shook her head. She knew that they
had a tough decision to make!

Look Closely

The problem in this passage
is that Jill surprises Stan by
wanting to try something new.
To figure out how the problem
is solved, read closely for
how things turn out for the
characters.

1   **Think about how the author organized the information in the passage.
Complete the timeline with ONE detail from the passage.**

Stan and Jill knead clay to make it soft.	→		→	The clay is baked in a kiln.	→	The clay is glazed.

Explain why this detail is important. Use evidence from the text.

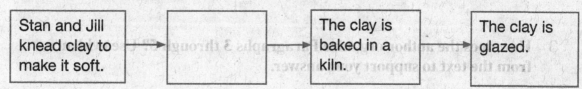

_____

_____

_____

_____

GO ON ▶

2 **Think about how the author organized the information in the passage.**
Complete the chart with ONE detail from the passage.

1. Jill asks Stan to try new projects.
2. They try pottery.
3.
4. They build a model plane.

Explain why this detail is important. Use evidence from the text.

_____

_____

_____

_____

3 **How does the author organize Paragraphs 3 through 5? Use evidence**
from the text to support your answer.

_____

_____

_____

_____

Writing and Research

Overview

Sometimes you will be asked to write an analysis of two or more pieces of writing. Sometimes digital and multimedia sources will be included. You may be asked to compare and contrast the selections. In this case, you would write about how the two sources are similar and how they are different. In all cases, you will be asked to use evidence from the texts to support your analysis and reflection.

Orient the Reader

Let the reader know what you are writing about. Write a beginning paragraph that clearly introduces your topic.

Create an Organizational Structure

Organize your essay so that related ideas are grouped to support your purpose.

• You might organize your essay by points: State a point and give an example from each text.

• You might organize your essay by topics: State several points and give examples from one text before moving on to the next text and addressing the same points.

Cite Evidence

Use examples from each text to support the ideas in your writing. For example, if you agree with one writer and disagree with the other, give examples and explain why.

Use Transitional Words and Phrases

Use a variety of transitional words and phrases to link ideas in your writing. Examples include *for example, in order to, in addition, because,* and *also.*

Precise Language

Use words that tell exactly what you mean. Also, use vocabulary that is specific to the topic. If you are not sure the reader will know a vocabulary word, define it.

Provide a Conclusion

Wrap up your writing with a concluding statement or paragraph. A conclusion should summarize the main points of the writing. You might also refer back to something important stated in the beginning of your writing.

Name _____ Date _____

Writing Practice

Read the two texts that follow. Take notes on each one. After you read, follow the directions to write an essay about what you have read.

The Brown Thrasher

The brown thrasher is the state bird of Georgia. Brown thrashers live in the southeastern United States, including Georgia, all year long. In the spring, some brown thrashers migrate as far north as Canada and as far west as Montana.

The brown thrasher is a fairly large bird, nearly a foot long. It has a long, thin bill. It uses its bill to grasp insects and seeds on the ground. Its back is brown but its belly is white with streaks or spots of black.

Brown thrashers usually make their nests just a few feet off the ground in thick, thorny bushes. The thorns help protect the birds against cats and other animals that prowl about. Thrashers will peck at any animal or human that seems to be attacking. So don't get too close.

It may be difficult to see brown thrashers in the thick bushes, but you have probably heard them. They are terrific singers. In fact, they sing more than 1,000 different songs. They often repeat a phrase, or short series of sounds. The next time you are outside and hear the sound of a bird you cannot see, look around to see if it is a brown thrasher.

How could multimedia help you to give more information in a report about the brown thrasher?

_____

_____

_____

The Live Oak Tree

The live oak is Georgia's state tree. This tree can grow up to 80 feet tall. Huge limbs extend from its short, thick trunk. Some of these limbs may bend close to the ground before angling upward. Then its leafy branches spread out wide. This creates a large canopy that provides welcome shade on a hot Georgia summer day.

The live oak is a hardy tree. Its roots are deep. Therefore, the tree can stand up to hurricanes and other storms that batter the coast along the Gulf of Mexico. The wood is strong. Shipbuilders used it for parts of the hulls of wooden ships in the 1700s and 1800s. In fact, in the War of 1812, a wooden warship called the USS *Constitution* survived battles partly because cannonballs couldn't blast their way through this strong wood.

Many live oaks are draped with another plant called Spanish moss. It's not really moss. It's a flowering plant that attaches itself to the branches of live oaks. The hanging stems of the Spanish moss take in rainwater as it falls. Seeds from the Spanish moss float on the wind and stick to other tree branches. That's how more Spanish moss grows.

So how do new live oak trees grow? The seeds of a live oak are acorns. An average tree might drop more than 2,000 acorns. Many of these rot on the ground or are eaten by animals. However, about 1 in every 10,000 acorns grows into a new tree.

Why does the writer include the story about the USS *Constitution*?

_____

_____

_____

GO ON ▶

You have read two texts about plants and animals in Georgia. Think about the information in each text. Recall any experiences you may have had with either of these living things.

Write an essay about the brown thrasher and live oak tree. Include descriptions of these living things and summarize why they are symbols of the state of Georgia. Use this space to plan your writing. Write your essay on a separate sheet of paper in your best cursive handwriting. Remember to use textual evidence to support your ideas.

Planning

_____

_____

_____

_____

_____

_____

_____

_____

_____

_____

STOP

Name _____ Date _____

Problem and Solution

How to Analyze the Text

The selection *Harvesting Hope* tells about the poor living conditions and unfair treatment that people faced while working on farms in California. Cesar Chavez helped solve these problems. He started the National Farm Workers Association and led a march to the California state capitol.

Authors often describe a **problem and solution** in their writings. The problem may be one that the author sees in the community, such as the need for more schools. Other times, an author will write about a problem in the world at large, such as global warming. The author will then give ideas for the ways that the problem can be solved. Plenty of facts, reasons, and examples are used to support the author's thoughts about both the problem and solutions.

GO ON ▶

Name _____ Date _____

Apply to Text

Read the passage below and answer the questions that follow.

Protect the Manatees

1   Manatees are harmless water mammals. These
gentle giants are shaped like fat torpedoes and look like
walruses without tusks. Adult manatees can weigh over
2,000 pounds. They swim slowly near the shore, eating
sea grass and other plants. An adult can eat 150 pounds
of plants a day!

2   The manatee population today is small. There
are only about 3,000 manatees in the United States.
Manatees are in danger of disappearing forever. One
reason is that they only live in certain places. They like
warm shallow waters, mostly around Florida and in the
Gulf of Mexico. Another reason is that the population
grows slowly. Females usually give birth to one baby
every two to five years.

3   Manatees are also endangered because of humans.
Speedboats are dangerous to manatees. Manatees swim
slowly and close to the surface. The blades of a fast-
moving motorboat can cause serious injury or death.
Humans also make the waters where manatees live less
clean. Pollution threatens their survival.

4   There are ways that people can help keep manatees
safe. Fast-moving boats can't see manatees until it is
too late. Therefore, slow-speed zones in areas where
manatees live would help protect them. Another idea is
for boaters to place propeller guards on their boats.

Look Closely

Look for a problem that
the author states near the
beginning of the passage.
Then look for the reasons the
author describes.

Look Closely

Pay close attention to how
the author uses facts and
examples to describe the
problem.

Look Closely

Carefully read each topic
sentence so you will know
when the author moves from
describing the problem to
talking about solutions.

Name _____ Date _____

5   People can also protect the water where manatees live. They can limit building on nearby land and reduce chemicals that run into the water. Protecting manatees in these ways may help ensure that these interesting and gentle creatures will be around for a long time to come.

> **Look Closely**
>
> Look for what the author says about people helping to solve the problem.

1 **Which sentence from the passage BEST states the problem that manatees face?**

   A   Adult manatees can weigh over 2,000 pounds.

   B   Manatees swim slowly and close to the surface.

   C   Manatees are in danger of disappearing forever.

   D   Females usually give birth to one baby every two to five years.

> **Look Closely**
>
> Reread the beginning of the passage to identify the main problem. Then review the reasons.

2 **Which of the following is NOT a reason for the problem that manatees face?**

   A   They only eat plants.

   B   They live only in certain places.

   C   They can be injured or killed by boats.

   D   Humans pollute the waters where manatees live.

3 **According to the author, which is one solution to the manatees' problems?**

   A   Observe manatees more closely.

   B   Remove fast-moving blades from motor boats.

   C   Create ways for manatees to give birth more often.

   D   Establish slow-speed zones in areas where manatees live.

> **Look Closely**
>
> Reread the part of the passage that discusses solutions.

1 Ⓐ Ⓑ Ⓒ Ⓓ

2 Ⓐ Ⓑ Ⓒ Ⓓ

3 Ⓐ Ⓑ Ⓒ Ⓓ

GO ON ▶

69

Grade 4, Unit 4: Lesson 19

Read the letter below and answer the questions that follow.

Pollution in Our Parks

Dear Editor,

1   Our city parks used to provide beautiful places to take a walk, enjoy nature, or have a picnic. Unfortunately, I have noticed a change in our parks over the past few years. Now the parks are littered with trash, including old cans, wrappers, and broken glass. Why has this change occurred? One reason is that there are only a few trash cans at each park, and they fill up quickly. When this happens, people leave their garbage on the ground. It also doesn't help that cuts to the city budget have reduced the number of workers who take care of the parks.

2   There are some steps that we can take to end the pollution in our parks. If the trash cans are full, visitors can put their trash in a bag and throw it away at home. People can also organize clean-up days for the parks in their neighborhoods. Last, people can vote in the next election to increase the amount of money that goes into the city's parks services department.

3   Everyone wants to enjoy our city parks. So, let's work together to make them beautiful again!

4 **What is the MAIN problem that the author describes in the letter?**

   A   There are not enough trash cans in the city parks.

   B   There is no place in the city to have a picnic.

   C   The city had to make cuts to its budget.

   D   The city parks are littered with trash.

> **Look Closely**
>
> Read and think about the main point that the author is making.

5 **Which solution is NOT suggested by the author?**

   A   voting to put more money into park services

   B   buying more sweepers for the parks

   C   organizing park clean-up days

   D   throwing trash away at home

> **Look Closely**
>
> Reread the author's solutions.

4 Ⓐ Ⓑ Ⓒ Ⓓ
5 Ⓐ Ⓑ Ⓒ Ⓓ

STOP ⬤

Writing to Narrate

Overview

Sometimes you will be asked to complete a **narrative** task. This means that you will write a story. You may be asked to write about something that you make up. You may be asked to write about something that actually happened. Sometimes you will be asked to write about only a part of a narrative, such as adding a beginning or an ending to a story. Your narrative writing should do the following:

Orient the Reader

Establish a situation. Make sure readers know what is happening and where it takes place. Introduce and describe the characters. You may want to use a narrator to tell the story. Be sure to organize your writing so that the reader can follow along as the events unfold.

Use Dialogue and Description

Use dialogue so that the reader knows what the different characters say to one another and how they respond to situations. Describe what the characters see and do and how they feel about what is happening.

Use Transitional Words and Phrases

Use transitional words to connect different parts of a story. Some transitional words show sequence, such as *In the beginning, first, second, then*, and *last*. These transitions will help your reader understand the order of events.

Use Concrete Words and Sensory Details

Use concrete words (*downpour* instead of *rain*, for example) and sensory details (words that appeal to the five senses: *plop, jagged*, and *crunchy*, for example) to help readers experience what you are describing.

Provide a Conclusion

Wrap up your writing with an ending or conclusion that makes sense based on what happens with the characters. If there is a problem that a character must solve, make sure you explain the solution in detail so your readers won't be confused about what happened.

GO ON ▶

Name _____ Date _____

Writing Practice

Read the text below. Then complete the task that follows.

Big Adventure at Red Top

Tamara jumped up and reached high into the air.

"I got it!" she exclaimed. She grabbed the small, spongy football by her fingertips before hitting the water with a splash.

"Nice catch!" yelled her brother Bryce.

Tamara laughed and stood up in the knee-deep water. What a perfect day to be at the beach, she thought. Tamara and her little brother Bryce were spending the day with their family at Red Top Mountain State Park, not far from Atlanta. The cool water felt good on this hot summer Saturday.

Tamara and Bryce continued tossing the ball for a while. Then they decided to build a sand castle on the beach.

"Let's make the biggest sand castle ever!" said Bryce as he clawed into the wet sand near the water's edge. They dug into the sand and piled it high. They used a toy shovel and twigs to carve the sand into four towers connected by walls. Then they sat back and admired their work. "Okay, now we have to dig the moat," said Bryce excitedly.

They started using their hands to scoop out a small ditch around the castle. About halfway around, Tamara suddenly stopped. Something felt different. Instead of soft sand, her fingers scraped against something hard and smooth. "Hey, what's this?" She brushed away some sand. Something glistened and sparkled in the bright sunshine.

In the story, Tamara and Bryce find something interesting in the sand. Is it a small object? Is it part of something bigger? Is it something valuable? Does it lead to an adventure? Think about some of the possibilities.

Write an ending for the story by adding details to tell what happens next. Plan and write your ending on separate sheets of paper.

STOP

Context Clues and Multiple-Meaning Words

Skill Overview

In *The World According to Humphrey,* you might have read words you didn't know, such as *bombarded, feats,* or *blissfully.* What did you do to figure out the meanings of those words?

When you read, you sometimes see unknown words or phrases. To find the meanings, you can search for **context clues**, or clues in nearby words or sentences. Context clues might:

- have the same or almost the same meaning as an unknown word

- have the opposite meaning as an unknown word

- explain, give examples of, or describe an unknown word

Read this example.

> The truck unloaded an <u>immense</u> mound of dirt in the garden. The pile was just huge!

The word *immense* means almost the same thing as *huge.*

Sometimes words used together make an expression you have never heard. Read this example.

> Celia's office was a <u>dog-eat-dog world</u>. Everyone there was very competitive.

Context clues tell you that a *dog-eat-dog world* means a place where people compete with each other and care only about their own success.

Context clues can help you figure out multiple-meaning words. A **multiple-meaning word** has more than one meaning.

> Twenty kids were <u>present</u> for the party. Everyone who came brought Jorge a nice <u>present</u>.

In the first sentence, *present* means "in attendance" or "there." In the second sentence, *present* means "gift."

GO ON ▶

Apply to Text

Read the passage below and answer the questions that follow.

Queen of the House

1   Violet the cat was the queen of the house. Her owner, Barbara, spoiled her rotten. Barbara showered her with gifts, including toy mice and big balls of yarn, her favorite kitty treats, and soft collars in a rainbow of colors.

2   Even though Violet had her own velvety bed, complete with little pillows and blankets, she slept wherever she desired. She curled up on top of the couch or sprawled out in the middle of the living room rug. At night, she always slept with Barbara, right smack in the middle of the bed. One of her favorite places to relax was on her owner's lap. Barbara would stroke the soft fur between her ears, and she would purr contentedly and smile.

3   The only thing that could disturb Violet's peace of mind was a visit from Melrose, the giant orange cat who lived next door. Melrose's owner was away a lot, so Barbara babysat him. Melrose always gobbled down Violet's food as well as his own. He sat in Violet's favorite sunny spot on the windowsill.

4   One day, Violet decided she had had enough of Melrose. When Barbara woke up that morning, she found Melrose in the windowsill. Violet, though, had vanished. She was nowhere to be found. Barbara couldn't account for it. She was frantic with worry, looking in every cabinet and closet, and under every bed and chair. Barbara went door to door, asking neighbors if they had seen her precious cat. No one had seen Violet.

5   Two days later, Barbara still had not found Violet. Melrose's owner came to take Melrose home and to thank Barbara for taking care of him. Barbara had just gone back in her house and closed the door when she recognized a familiar sound. It was Violet meowing at the door.

Look Closely

Look closely for clue words around the word *contentedly* for clues about its meaning.

Look Closely

Look for descriptions of what Barbara did for clues to the meaning of *vanished*.

6   Barbara opened the door and joyfully scooped up Violet, who purred loudly. Violet had been hiding in the garage, and she was hungry, cold, and tired. She was glad to be home again sitting in Barbara's warm lap and ruling the roost once more.

Look Closely

If a group of words like *ruling the roost* does not make sense, use clues from the passage to help you figure out the meaning of the expression.

1   What is the meaning of *contentedly* in the sentence?

Barbara would stroke the soft fur between her ears, and she would purr <u>contentedly</u> and smile.

A   angrily

B   happily

C   impatiently

D   loudly

Look Closely

Reread Paragraph 2 and notice how Violet acts when she is petted.

2   What is the meaning of the word *vanished*?

Violet, though, had <u>vanished</u>.

A   arrived

B   disappeared

C   discovered

D   observed

1 (A) (B) (C) (D)
2 (A) (B) (C) (D)

GO ON ▶

Use the information in the box below to answer the question.

> **account** *v.* **1.** to provide an explanation **2.** to analyze
> *n.* **3.** a record of debt and credit **4.** value, importance

3 Which definition of the word *account* is used in the sentence?

> Barbara couldn't <u>account</u> for it.

Look Closely
Look at how the word is used in the sentence. The definition you choose should be the same part of speech as the original word.

A definition 1

B definition 2

C definition 3

D definition 4

4 Which word from Paragraph 5 helps the reader understand the meaning of the word *recognized*?

A back

B closed

C familiar

D sound

3 Ⓐ Ⓑ Ⓒ Ⓓ

4 Ⓐ Ⓑ Ⓒ Ⓓ

STOP

Conclusions and Generalizations

How to Analyze the Text

In *I Could Do That!,* Esther invited influential people to her house and treated them well. She agreed with what they said. However, the author never directly states that Esther invited them so that she could convince them that women should get the right to vote. The reader can figure it out, though, using clues in the story. Esther saw a sign explaining that male citizens 21 and older could vote in Wyoming Territory for the first time. This and other clues help the reader conclude that Esther wants to get the men to help women gain the right to vote.

Authors do not always tell every detail. Instead, they give clues and let readers figure things out. When you use clues to figure out something that is not directly stated, you **draw a conclusion**. You can also **make a generalization** about what you read. A generalization states an overall truth that applies to the whole selection.

When you draw a conclusion or make a generalization, you must explain why you think as you do. Suppose that you tell a friend that the bus will come in five minutes. She might ask, "How do you know?" Maybe you have a schedule or rode that bus before. Either way, you have a reason for knowing and can support your idea.

The same is true when you give ideas about what you read. You use the title, events, and other details in the passage to support your conclusions and generalizations.

Clues from Story

Tom kicks a soccer ball and runs laps every day.

Tom kicks a goal at the end of the game.

Tom's teammates cheer and carry him off the field.

Conclusion

Tom kicked the winning goal.

Generalization

Hard work pays off.

GO ON ▶

Name _____ Date _____

Apply to Text

Read the passage below and answer the questions that follow.

Only One Choice

1   Ben had dreamed all his life about river rafting. His Aunt Molly went river rafting every chance she could get and described the thrill she felt riding the rough currents. She promised Ben that as soon as he was old enough to use an oar to wrestle through the water, she would take him with her.

2   That day had arrived! Ben had told everyone he knew that he was going, including his little sister Tori, who listened intently as he described the roaring rapids, her eyes wide. Ben told Tori that when she was old enough, they could all go on a river rafting adventure together. Ben took Tori on other adventures, like fishing trips to the creek. He showed her how to put the bait on a hook and reel in a fish.

3   On the big day, Ben was packing when he heard his mom yell, "Ben! Come quickly!" He raced downstairs and saw his little sister, Tori, sitting on the kitchen floor. She was holding her leg. His mother was grabbing her car keys.

4   "I fell off my bike, and now my leg hurts," Tori cried.

5   "Ben, I'm going to take Tori to the hospital," his mother explained. "I think she may have broken her leg. I already called Aunt Molly and she is on her way to pick you up. Can you go wait at the neighbor's house for her while I take Tori to the hospital?"

6   They locked up the house. Ben and his mom helped Tori get into the backseat of the car. Then Ben's mom got into the driver's seat. As she was about to start the engine, Ben made a decision.

7   "Mom, wait a second."

8   Ben got in the back seat next to Tori and said, "I think this is enough excitement for me today."

> **Look Closely**
>
> The key events and facts in a story can support your conclusions. What facts and events have you read about so far?

> **Look Closely**
>
> What conclusion does Ben make? What clues from the story support this conclusion? How does the title connect with this conclusion?

1 What conclusion can you draw from the meaning of the title "Only One Choice"? Use evidence from the text to support your answer.

_____

_____

_____

_____

_____

2 What conclusion can you draw about Ben's relationship with his sister Tori? Give TWO details from the passage to support your answer.

_____

_____

_____

_____

_____

3 Can you generalize that Ben likes to spend time outdoors based on the story? Give TWO details from the passage to support your answer.

_____

_____

_____

_____

_____

GO ON

4 **What generalization can you make about Ben's character? Give THREE details from the passage to support your answer.**

_____

_____

_____

_____

_____

5 **Do you think Ben will skip the rafting trip to be with his sister? Give TWO details from the passage to support your answer.**

_____

_____

_____

_____

_____

6 **What generalization can you make from this passage? Give TWO details from the passage to support your answer.**

_____

_____

_____

_____

_____

STOP

Prefixes

Skill Overview

Many words in English begin with groups of letters called prefixes. A **prefix** can be attached to the beginning of a word. Though prefixes are not usually words themselves, they do have meanings. Adding a prefix changes the meaning of the base word or the root word. You saw a few words with prefixes in the passage *The Ever-Living Tree*.

Three common prefixes are *pre-*, *inter-*, and *ex-*.

The prefix *pre-* means "before." Examples of words with this prefix include:

- *prehistory*. This word means *before history*, or *before people started recording what happened in the world*.
- *pregame*. This word usually refers to programs and events that take place *before a game*.
- *predict*. This word comes from *pre-* and the root word *dict*. This root *dict* means *say* or *tell*, so to *predict* is to *say before*, or tell what will happen in the future.

The prefix *inter-* usually means "between" or "among." Examples include:

- *international*. A nation is a country, so *international* means *between countries* or *having to do with more than one country*.
- *interaction*. An *interaction* is an *activity* or *communication between or among* two or more people.

Finally, the prefix *ex-* often means "out" or "outside." An example is:

- *exclude*. The prefix *ex-* means *out*, and the root word *clude* means to shut or close. To *exclude* someone is to *shut them out* or *leave them out*.

Sometimes the meaning of a word with one of these prefixes is easy to see. Sometimes you have to think a bit to see how the prefix affects the word's meaning. If a meaning isn't obvious, context clues can help you discover exactly what the word means.

GO ON ▶

Name _____ Date _____

Skill Practice

Read the passage below and answer the questions that follow.

Freddy's Future Home

1 "I have a question for you," said Freddy to his best friend, Micah. The boys were on the bus heading to their after-school art class. "If you could live anywhere at all—I mean, *anywhere*—where would it be?"

2 Micah wrinkled his nose. "That's a good question," he began. "I like the beach, and I like the mountains, but if I could live anywhere in the entire world—"

3 "Well, see, I wouldn't live *in* the world," Freddy said, interrupting Micah as the bus stopped for a traffic light. "I would live in space, in a space colony on Mars, or on Neptune, or maybe on Jupiter. That would be amazingly cool—don't you think it would be exciting?"

4 "Um—" Micah began.

5 "I know there's no oxygen on Mars," Freddy said, "but that shouldn't be a problem. All you need to do is build a huge dome, and then you prepare for people to live there by filling the dome with regular air. The roof and the walls of the dome keep the oxygen inside so that people can inhale and exhale just the way we do on Earth."

6 "Well, the problem is—" said Micah.

7 "Jupiter would be a lot tougher than Mars, I admit it," said Freddy, paying no attention to his friend. "Jupiter is made out of hot gas and doesn't have any land at all. You'd have to have a dome that could float extremely well on the vapor." Freddy pointed at a truck parked at a nearby intersection. "But they can build vehicles and computer chips and other complicated things, right?"

8 Micah started to speak, but Freddy just kept going. "So why couldn't they make a dome that wouldn't be affected by gas?" he demanded. "You just have to take a few precautions to make sure it wouldn't burn up or anything."

9 "Freddy," Micah said, "I think—"

Look Closely

The word <u>interrupt</u> begins with the prefix *inter-*. How does knowing the meaning of the prefix *inter-* help you understand the meaning of the word *interrupting*?

Look Closely

Look for words with prefixes that mean *before, between,* or *out.*

Look Closely

What words in Paragraphs 7 and 8 have prefixes? What do the prefixes mean? What do the words mean?

10   "I know what you're going to say, Micah," Freddy
said with a grin. "You're going to say it's impossible to
get to Jupiter. That's true now, but by the time we grow
up interplanetary travel will be real. There'll be rockets
going from Mercury to Saturn almost every day, and it
won't take more than a few weeks to get from here to
Jupiter."

11   Micah rolled his eyes. "Listen, Freddy—" he began.

12   "See, the problem with you, Micah, is that you don't
think big," said Freddy, punching his friend lightly
on the arm. "All you dream about is living on a beach
somewhere and climbing mountains in your spare time,
but I think big—all the way to Jupiter!" He pumped his
fist. "Jupiter, here I come!" he sang. "I'll send you a
postcard when I get there."

13   "That may be quite a while," Micah said. He grinned
and elbowed his friend in the ribs, then pointed to a
nearby street sign. "We passed the stop for art class
almost a mile ago, but you were too busy talking to
notice. If you don't know when to exit the bus, I don't
see how you can ever take a trip to Jupiter!"

1   **Based on the prefix *ex-*, what is the meaning of *exhale*?**

> "The roof and the walls of the dome keep the oxygen
> inside so that people can inhale and <u>exhale</u> just the way
> we do on Earth."

A   breathe in

B   breathe out

C   jump up and down

D   throw things away

Look Closely

Think about the prefix *ex-*.
Also think about what Freddy
is discussing when he uses
this word.

1 Ⓐ Ⓑ Ⓒ Ⓓ

GO ON ▶

2 Which word from the passage means "a place where two or more streets come together"?

Look Closely

Reread Paragraph 7 and look for prefixes and clue words to help you.

A   attention

B   extremely

C   intersection

D   vapor

3 Which words in the passage suggest doing something BEFORE doing something else?

Look Closely

What prefix means "before"? Reread the sentences with these words to make sure the meaning makes sense.

A   exit, exciting

B   interrupt, inhale

C   punching, elbowed

D   prepare, precautions

4 Based on the prefix *inter-*, what is the meaning of *interplanetary travel*?

"That's true now, but by the time we grow up interplanetary travel will be real."

A   going between two or more planets

B   going to the center of Mars or Jupiter

C   going from one city or town to another

D   going from the North Pole to the South Pole

2 Ⓐ Ⓑ Ⓒ Ⓓ
3 Ⓐ Ⓑ Ⓒ Ⓓ
4 Ⓐ Ⓑ Ⓒ Ⓓ

STOP 🛑

Name _____ Date _____

Language Arts

Skill Overview

You can use adjectives and adverbs to make your writing clearer and more interesting. An **adjective** is a word that describes a noun or pronoun. Adjectives tell what kind, how many, and which one. *Tall, stormy, noisy,* and *crowded* are examples of adjectives.

An **adverb** tells about a verb. An adverb tells how, when, or where. *Quickly, happily,* and *recently* are examples of adverbs.

Commas tell readers when to stop and pause. We use commas in different ways when writing.

Separate words in a series	The flag is red, white, and blue.
Separate a date and its year	July 22, 2013
Separate a city and state names	Atlanta, GA
Following the greeting and closing of a friendly letter	Dear Rudy, Love, Anna

An **abbreviation** is a shortened form of a word. Many abbreviations begin with a capital letter and end with a period. Abbreviations can be used in addresses to write street names and state names:

Street	*St.*	Avenue	*Ave.*	Road	*Rd.*
Georgia	*GA*	New York	*NY*	Texas	*TX*

Abbreviations can be used to write days and months:

Monday	*Mon.*	Tuesday	*Tues.*	Friday	*Fri.*
January	*Jan.*	March	*Mar.*	December	*Dec.*

Abbreviations can also be used for people:

Mister	*Mr.*	Doctor	*Dr.*	Senior	*Sr.*

GO ON

Name _____ Date _____

Apply to Text

Read the passage below and answer the questions that follow.

1 **Which sentence uses a comma correctly?**

A   Tamika has history, English, and, science classes today.

B   Tamika has history English and science classes today.

C   Tamika has history, English, and science, classes today.

D   Tamika has history, English, and science classes today.

2 **What is the correct way to write the underlined part of the sentence?**

> Of the three mountains, Rob climbed the one with the
> <u>highly peak</u>.

A   mostly high peak

B   higher peak

C   highest peak

D   most higher

3 **What is the correct way to write the abbreviation for the underlined name?**

> I have an appointment with <u>Doct. Richards</u> today.

A   Dr. Richards

B   Dt. Richards

C   Do. Richards

D   Dc. Richards

1 Ⓐ Ⓑ Ⓒ Ⓓ

2 Ⓐ Ⓑ Ⓒ Ⓓ

3 Ⓐ Ⓑ Ⓒ Ⓓ   STOP

Writing to Inform

Overview

Sometimes you will be asked to complete an **informative** task. This means writing about a topic or an idea. You may be asked to give information about a topic based on two or more sources of information that you have read. You may be asked to explain how to do something or how something works. Your informative texts should do the following:

Introduce the Topic and Organize Information

Introduce the topic and present information in a way that makes sense. Decide whether you will use illustrations or other visual elements. Consider whether section headings or numbers would help readers locate information or follow steps in a sequence. For example, some informative writing uses numbers to order the steps a person should follow.

Develop the Topic with Details and Examples

Organize and present details and examples compiled from your research. Include only those details and examples that clearly relate to your topic. Use facts, definitions, quotations, and illustrations and other visual elements to develop your topic.

Link Ideas

Use transitional words to connect sentences and paragraphs. Transitional words and phrases (*except, as well as, besides, if, first,* and *especially,* for example) link ideas in a meaningful way and help readers understand your writing.

Use Precise Language

Use precise language by selecting words with specific meanings that relate to the topic (*take all five beans* instead of *take the beans,* for example). Think about the terms and vocabulary you plan to use and consider whether you should define certain terms so readers will understand the points you are making.

Provide a Concluding Statement or Section

Wrap up your writing with a concluding statement or paragraph that restates your major point or points. Think about the most important idea you want to get across and create a summary or final sentence that readers will remember.

GO ON

Name _____ Date _____

Writing Practice

Read the two texts. Take notes on each one. Then complete the task that follows.

A World of Careers

What would you like to be when you grow up? It can be difficult to decide what career you might want to have some day. You have to ask yourself lots of questions. What do I like to do? What am I good at? What kind of education do I need for different jobs? How much money can I earn in different jobs? To get a better idea of possible careers, take a look at the chart below. It shows just a few of the many careers that are likely to provide good opportunities for employment in the future.

Career	Description	Typical Salary After Some Experience	Education Required
Dentist	Helps people by providing medical care for people's gums and teeth	$140,000	bachelor's degree and dental school
Registered Nurse	Works in hospitals, doctor's offices, and almost any other type of facility that provides medical care	$65,000	associate degree or bachelor's degree in science
Computer Systems Analyst	Makes sure that a company's computers and computer programs (software) are used in the most efficient and helpful way	$78,000	bachelor's degree
Database Administrator	Sets up the database for the company and then makes changes and upgrades as needed	$75,000	bachelor's degree in computer-related field
Web Developer	Creates the design and layout of websites	$75,000	technical skills and experience or a bachelor's degree
Interpreter and Translator	Translates one language to another; this can include translating oral speech to sign language at conferences or translating written work from one language to another	$44,000	fluency in at least two languages; sometimes certification and a bachelor's degree

What other questions might you ask yourself before choosing a career?

Education and Job Training

Some people begin working full-time as soon as they graduate from high school. Many other people choose to continue their education. Here are some ways you can continue your education after high school so that you get the career you want.

Certificate Programs These programs prepare people for careers that do not need a college degree. In some states people must take tests to show they are qualified to work in a certain field. Such fields include cooking, mechanics, and carpentry.

Associate Degree Programs A person can earn an associate degree after taking about 20 college courses. It takes about two years to get an associate degree. Many people go to a community college for this degree because it is cheaper than a four-year college. Other people choose to get an associate degree because that is all they need for their career.

Bachelor's Degree Programs Four-year colleges and universities offer bachelor's degrees. Some courses that students take are general in nature. Students can choose from lots of different subjects. Other courses must be in the student's area of study.

Postgraduate Degree Programs When a person wants to get more education in the same field, he or she can get a master's degree or a doctorate. Some careers require this level of study or knowledge within the field.

What is the difference between an associate degree and a bachelor's degree?

_____

_____

_____

GO ON ▶

The texts you have read describe different careers and different educational choices. Look at the list of careers and decide which of these is most interesting to you.

Write an informative essay describing the career that interests you most. Explain why you are interested in that career. If none of the careers interest you, explain why. Include information from both of the texts in your essay. Use the space below to plan your essay. Write your informative text on a separate sheet of paper.

Planning

_____

_____

_____

_____

_____

_____

_____

_____

_____

STOP

Name _____ Date _____

Reading Practice Test

Part 1

Read the passage below and answer the questions that follow.

Mystery Maps

1   Jayla woke up on a sunny Saturday morning, but she did not feel like getting out of bed. She had her own room now and didn't have to share with her pesky little brother, so what was the problem? Jayla's family had moved all the way across the country five weeks ago, and making new friends at school was turning out to be harder than she thought it would be.

2   The move had come in the middle of the year, so the kids at school already had their friends. They weren't looking to make new ones. Since she was the odd one out, they hadn't given her much of a chance. They weren't mean or anything; they just sort of ignored her.

3   Jayla was thinking about her old friends when her mom called her down to breakfast. Jayla was about to say that she didn't want anything when her mom surprised her by saying, "Come down. There's something for you under the door."

4   An envelope with Jayla's name on it had been found by the door with the morning newspaper. Confused, and a little bit excited for the first time in a while, Jayla ripped it open and found a strange piece of paper inside. It was torn at the edges and had dotted lines and squiggly shapes. She didn't know what to make of it.

5   Jayla's brother said, "It looks like some kind of map of our neighborhood."

6   "You're right," replied Jayla. "There's a big X on it where it looks like the park should be."

7   "What else do you see?" Mom asked.

8   Jayla looked more carefully. "It shows a time, 12:00 P.M., and a picture of something that looks like a jar of peanut butter."

9   "Well," Mom said, "you'd better hurry if you're going to make it to the park by 12. And here is a jar of peanut butter, just in case."

10   Jayla dressed quickly, put the peanut butter in her backpack, and jumped on her bike. She arrived at the park just a minute before noon. When she got there, she saw another girl about her age, sitting on a picnic table, looking as confused as she was.

11   "Hi," she said. "I'm Raina. I've seen you at school. You're new around here, right?"

GO ON ▶

12   The girls talked for a few minutes about how they had both received a map under the door that morning and showed up at the park. Jayla brought peanut butter, and Raina had a jar of jelly. They both thought that was bizarre, and it really made them wonder what was going on. As they talked, another girl arrived on a bike with a big smile on her face.

13   "You both made it!" she exclaimed. "Hi Raina. Hi Jayla, I'm Sue. Raina and I are friends at school and I've seen you in class. I thought it would be nice to meet you, so I worked out this unexpected way that we could all get together."

14   Raina laughed. "Sue, I thought I had found a treasure map that was going to lead me to a great treasure!"

15   "It did," said Sue. "A new friend is a true treasure."

16   Sue looked down at the table and saw the peanut butter and jelly. As she opened her backpack, she said, "I see you figured out the clues about what to bring. I brought the bread!" Sue, Raina, and Jayla made sandwiches together. While they talked during the picnic, Jayla realized that, for the first time since her family had moved, it would be easy to get up for school on Monday.

1   **What is a synonym for *bizarre* in this sentence from Paragraph 12?**

> They both thought that was bizarre, and it really made them wonder what was going on.

   A   exciting

   B   sad

   C   strange

   D   wonderful

2   **Why is the setting of a new town important to the story?**

   A   Jayla likes living in her new town.

   B   Jayla has her own room in the new house.

   C   Jayla received a map under the door.

   D   Jayla has trouble making friends in her new school.

3 **What happens AFTER Jayla rides her bike to the park?**

A   She puts a jar of peanut butter into her backpack.

B   She meets Raina, a girl from her new school.

C   Her mother calls her down for breakfast.

D   Her brother tells her that the piece of paper has a map of the neighborhood.

4 **How is Jayla's problem solved?**

A   Jayla's mother tells her they will move back to their old town.

B   Jayla realizes that friendship is not important.

C   Jayla starts to become friends with Raina and Sue.

D   Jayla finally gets to eat a sandwich.

5 **Based on what happens in the passage, what will MOST LIKELY happen in the future?**

A   Jayla will start to enjoy her new town.

B   Jayla will have to share a room with her little brother.

C   Raina and Sue will ignore Jayla at school.

D   Jayla's old friends will visit her.

6 **Why did the author MOST LIKELY write this passage?**

A   to inform the reader of real events

B   to entertain the reader with a story

C   to convince the reader to make new friends

D   to give facts about making new friends

GO ON ▶

Read the journal entry below and answer the questions that follow.

September 28, 2013

(1) Today I woke up early and jumped out of bed right away. (2) I dressed quickly in shorts, a t-shirt, and my tennis shoes. (3) As soon as I was dressed, I ran downstairs and looked out the front windows. (4) I couldn't wait for my grandma to show up! (5) We were going to go to the zoo. (6) We has enjoyed many other days together. (7) Sinse we always have spectacular outings, I knew today would be just as special.

(8) My mom made me sit down and eat breakfast. (9) I was so excited that I couldn't barely eat nothing. (10) As soon as I heard a car pulling up, I raced to the front door. (11) I yelled, "Mom, Yaya's here!"

(12) After Yaya hugged mom and me, Yaya and I got into the car to begin our day of fun. (13) Sang songs as she drove to the zoo.

(14) At the zoo, I ran to see the snakes first. (15) Afterward, I led Yaya all around the zoo to see tigers, elephants, alligators, polar bears, and many other animals. (16) She didn't seem to like the snakes and alligators, but she liked to watch the polar bears swim.

(17) Then we saw a special performance by a group of actors. (18) They put on plaze about animals, and the play we watched was about snakes. (19) It was really cool!

(20) Finally, Yaya drove me home. (21) Before she left, she pulled a bag from her purse. (22) She had bought me a book about snakes. (23) I thanked her with a big hug. (24) What a great surprise

7 Which is the correct abbreviation for the underlined word?

September 28, 2013

A Spt.

B Septem.

C Sept.

D Sptm.

8   What is the correct way to write the date at the top of the entry?

    A   September, 28, 2013

    B   September, 28 2013

    C   September 28 2013

    D   September 28, 2013

9   Which is the BEST way to write the underlined part of the sentence?

> We <u>has enjoyed</u> many other days together.

    A   have enjoyed

    B   enjoys

    C   enjoying

    D   have enjoys

10   Which is the correct way to write the underlined word?

> They put on <u>plaze</u> about animals, and the play we watched was about snakes.

    A   playes

    B   plais

    C   plays

    D   place

GO ON ▶

Name _____ Date _____

11　**What is the correct way to write Sentence 13?**

> Sang songs as she drove to the zoo.

A　Sang songs as they drove to the zoo.

B　We sang songs as she drove to the zoo.

C　We singing songs as she drove to the zoo.

D　And singing songs as she drove to the zoo.

12　**The sentence below has a spelling error. Which of the underlined words in the sentence is spelled incorrectly?**

> Sinse we always have spectacular outings, I knew today would be just as special.

A　sinse

B　spectacular

C　would

D　special

13　**Which is the correct way to write the underlined part of the sentence?**

> I was so excited that I couldn't barely eat nothing.

A　could barely eat anything

B　could not barely eat nothing

C　couldn't barely eat everything

D　couldn't eat nothing

Name _____ Date _____

14 **Which sentence is punctuated correctly?**

A   What a great surprise,

B   What a great surprise?

C   What a great surprise;

D   What a great surprise!

GO ON

Read the passage below and answer the questions that follow.

Sunken Treasure

A Voyage from Cuba to Spain

1   It was early July 1715. General Don Juan Esteban de Ubilla had four ships in his New Spain fleet, including the *Urca de Lima*. This ship had a flat bottom and a large cargo area that held crates of chocolate and vanilla. The plan was for Ubilla's fleet to travel from Havana, Cuba, to Spain with the six ships of the Tierra Firme fleet. Together, the fleets would carry their goods, along with $15 million worth of gold and silver, back to Spain. Ubilla knew that many storms hit during the summer, and that this was not a good time to set sail. He also knew that King Philip V of Spain needed the fleets' supplies to pay for his wars. With this in mind, Ubilla decided that the fleets would not wait to make the voyage back to Spain. They left Havana, Cuba, on July 24, 1715.

An Easy Voyage Turns Rough

2   During the first days of the voyage, the two fleets made their way along the east coast of Florida. Ubilla and the fleets' crews were pleasantly surprised by the mild, sunny weather, and they thought they'd have an easy voyage ahead. Soon, however, everything began to change. The waves that gently lapped against their ships turned to large swells. A moist blanket of air filled the sky. Strong winds pushed 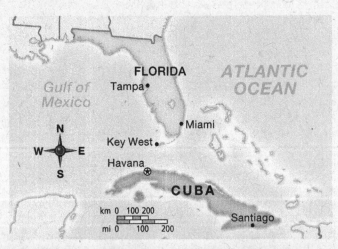 the fleets closer to the shallow reefs of the shoreline. The men knew that the weather would likely get worse, but there was little they could do. On July 31, their fears came true. A huge storm swept through the area, sinking all of the ships in the two fleets.

Recovering the Sunken Treasure

3   News of the sunken ships, and their sunken treasure, spread like wildfire. Boats from Havana and St. Augustine, Florida, quickly made their way to the area. They brought food and other supplies to the survivors. They also brought equipment that would help them recover the sunken treasure. This proved to be a difficult job. Wreckage from the fleets littered over 30 miles of the coastline.

4   The *Urca de Lima* was the only ship that had not completely broken apart. It sank in shallow water, and its flat bottom saved most of its riches from being swept

away. The men went to the *Urca de Lima* first and recovered much of the cargo that she carried. They then moved onto the other ships in the fleet. The men spent several months trying to recover all of the Spanish ships' sunken treasure. By 1716, they gave up, even though half of the treasure still lay on the bottom of the ocean floor.

Rediscovering the *Urca de Lima*

5   Over time, people forgot about the sunken fleets. Then, in 1928, treasure hunters rediscovered the *Urca de Lima*. Like the Spanish sailors before them, the treasure hunters explored the site with the hope that they would find something valuable. For the next 50 years, divers and adventurers from all over the world visited the *Urca de Lima*. Finally, in the 1980s, the state of Florida stopped allowing people to recover items from the sunken ship. Instead, the state opened the *Urca de Lima* to the public. It became Florida's first Underwater Archaeological Preserve.

6   Today, tourists and divers continue to explore the *Urca de Lima*. Its wreckage lies 200 yards offshore near Fort Pierce. As people visit this historic site, they may think about Ubilla's bad decision. But, without that decision, the state of Florida may not have one of its greatest treasures—the only surviving ship from the New Spain fleet of 1715.

15   **What is the meaning of the underlined word?**

> Then, in 1928, treasure hunters <u>rediscovered</u> the *Urca de Lima*.

   A   discovered before

   B   discovered again

   C   discovered after

   D   able to discover

16   **Which section of the article tells about the storm that sank the ships?**

   A   A Voyage from Cuba to Spain

   B   An Easy Voyage Turns Rough

   C   Recovering the Sunken Treasure

   D   Rediscovering the *Urca de Lima*

GO ON

17 **Which event belongs in the empty box in the chart?**

1.	Ubilla decides to make the voyage back to Spain.
2.	The fleets sink.
3.	
4.	The state of Florida opens the *Urca de Lima* site to the public.

A   The fleets leave from Havana, Cuba.

B   The fleets travel along the east coast of Florida.

C   People recover cargo items from the *Urca de Lima*.

D   The state of Florida opens an Underwater Archaeological Preserve.

18 **Which would be the BEST reference to use to see other maps of Cuba and Florida?**

A   dictionary

B   encyclopedia

C   atlas

D   thesaurus

19 **Why was it so difficult to recover the sunken treasure?**

A   The large storms kept coming.

B   The wreck covered more than thirty miles of coast line.

C   Too many people were searching.

D   Many treasure hunters just gave up.

20   Which would be the BEST source of more information about Don Juan Esteban de Ubilla?

A   Web site titled *Kings and Queens of Spain*

B   journal titled *Modern Spanish Life*

C   picture book titled *All About Ships*

D   book titled *Spanish Generals of the 1700s*

21   Which source could NOT have been used in the early 1900s to research information for a report about the *Urca de Lima*?

A   a book about the *Urca de Lima*

B   an online encyclopedia article about the *Urca de Lima*

C   a newspaper article about the *Urca de Lima*

D   a letter written by someone who tried to recover treasure from the *Urca de Lima*

22   What is the meaning of the word *recover*?

> They also brought equipment that would help them recover the sunken treasure.

A   to feel better

B   to use again

C   to find something that is lost

D   to place something over another item

GO ON ▶

Read the poem below and answer the questions that follow.

An Unwelcome Guest

A wild, gray guest blows into town
And people pull their windows down.
Rushing up and down the streets,
She shoves at everyone she meets.

5   They race inside and slam their doors,
As this angry guest shrieks and roars.
"This storm," they cry, "is more than rain!
It has become a hurricane!"

Denied our hospitality,
10   The wild guest tore through our city,
Ripped branches off the sides of trees
And flung them on the street like skis.

Her greenish clouds swirled until they burst.
Her manners were the very worst!
15   Rain poured down like water from a faucet.
Streets were streams, and if your car was there, you lost it.

After putting out every city light
And keeping us awake all night,
The storm blew out of town (she had no bags to pack)
20   But what a mess she left! We'll never ask her back.

23   **In the third stanza, to what does the speaker compare tree branches?**

    A   a wild guest

    B   skis

    C   a street

    D   the city

24   **The underlined words are an example of which figure of speech?**

> And <u>people pull</u> their windows down.

    A   alliteration

    B   repetition

    C   rhyme

    D   simile

25   **Who or what is the "wild, gray guest" in the poem?**

    A   an older person

    B   a strange traveler

    C   a car

    D   a hurricane

26   **What is the main idea of the poem?**

    A   The speaker enjoys the wind and rain.

    B   The speaker is excited about the storm.

    C   The speaker is fearful and upset about the storm.

    D   The speaker is glad the storm brought so much rain.

GO ON ▶

Read the passage below and answer the questions that follow.

Sleep

No one is really sure why the body needs sleep. But people who go without enough sleep for long periods of time become weak and sick. The body has trouble fighting off disease when it is tired. For reasons that are not yet clear, people who sleep too little also tend to gain weight. A possible reason is that one common response to being tired is overeating. Scientists say that sleeplessness can also lead to memory loss and difficulty making decisions. Sleeping is an important part of a healthful life. You should plan your day to give yourself plenty of time to sleep.

27 **What would be another good title for the paragraph?**

A Healthful Living

B Don't Lose Sleep

C How the Human Body Works

D Eating Healthfully

28 **Which sentence would make the BEST topic sentence for the paragraph?**

A Lack of sleep can lead to serious consequences.

B Some people stay up way too late.

C It is important to eat right every day.

D Sleeping too little can make people forgetful.

29 For which audience did the author MOST LIKELY write the paragraph?

    A   people who know why sleep is important

    B   people who get enough sleep

    C   scientists who want to know more about sleep

    D   people who need to know why they need more sleep

30 Which is the reason that the author MOST LIKELY wrote the paragraph?

    A   to entertain readers with a story

    B   to explain to readers how to get a good night's rest

    C   to persuade readers to do something that is good for them

    D   to inform readers about a scientific debate

GO ON ▶

Name _____ Date _____

31 Which sentence is written correctly?

   A   She walked to school more quick today than yesterday.

   B   She walked to school more quicker today than yesterday.

   C   She walked to school more quickly today than yesterday.

   D   She walked to school quicklier today than yesterday.

32 A student is giving a presentation to a group of classmates. Which behavior is MOST appropriate for the group of classmates?

   A   asking questions while the speaker is talking

   B   listening and taking notes during the presentation

   C   whispering questions to each other about the presentation

   D   doing homework

33 What belongs in the empty box in the chart?

Name	Age	Number of Books Read in March
Dina	10	8
Miguel	11	15
Douglas		12

   A   the title for a column

   B   the name of a student

   C   the number of books read

   D   the age of a student

34 In which chapter would you MOST LIKELY find information about the largest city in the state?

Chapter 1	Early History
Chapter 2	The Road to Statehood
Chapter 3	Georgia in the 21st Century
Chapter 4	Important Cities and Towns

A   Chapter 1

B   Chapter 2

C   Chapter 3

D   Chapter 4

35 A student is using this web to plan the first paragraph of a report about Georgia. Which of these belongs in the empty oval?

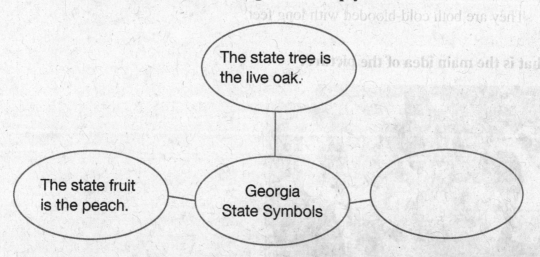

A   The live oak became Georgia's official state tree in 1937.

B   Georgia is north of Florida.

C   The state crop is the peanut.

D   The peach is also the state fruit of South Carolina.

GO ON ▶

36 According to the Venn diagram, how are frogs and toads the SAME?

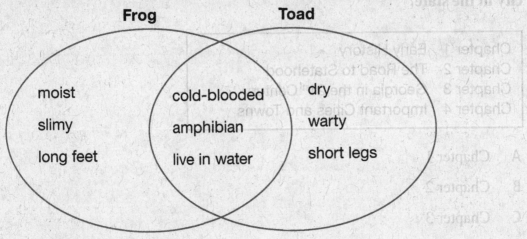

Frog   Toad

moist   cold-blooded   dry
slimy   amphibian   warty
long feet   live in water   short legs

A   They both have short legs.

B   They both live in water.

C   They are both amphibians with dry skin.

D   They are both cold-blooded with long feet.

37 What is the main idea of the picture?

A   A group of people plays in the mud.

B   People enjoy the weather on a nice day.

C   People work together to plant a tree.

D   A group of people digs for treasure.

38   **Which would be the BEST source for information about Georgia population changes from 1960 to the present?**

   A   personal memoirs of important people in Georgia's history

   B   U.S. government Web sites with census information

   C   any Web site resulting from a Web search about Georgia population

   D   magazines and newspapers from 1960

Part 2

Read the passage below and answer the questions that follow.

A Different Kind of Friday

1   Friday morning, the classroom was filled with outdoor tools. There were shovels, rakes, and hoes. The activity table had a box of garden gloves and small digging tools. There were also pinecones and a jar of peanut butter.

2   Aisha was the first student to enter the room that morning. She said to Mr. Agawa, "I have an idea how the tools and gloves might go together, but how do pinecones and peanut butter fit in this group?"

3   Her teacher grinned as he answered, "Don't worry, it will all make sense later."

4   Aisha heard a noise in the hallway and looked out. She was surprised to see Caleb and José pulling a wagon down the hall. Inside the wagon were heavy bags of rocks and planting soil.

5   As the boys pulled the wagon inside the classroom, José said, "Here are the bags you asked us to get from the back of your truck."

6   "What are these for?" asked Caleb. Mr. Agawa only grinned and directed the boys to the spot where he wanted the wagon.

7   Soon, the classroom was full of students. Mr. Agawa pointed out that today was the last Friday in April. It was the day when Arbor Day is celebrated in the United States. He told the students that it is common to plant a tree on that day. Mr. Agawa told his students that they were going to plant three small trees.

8   Mr. Agawa said that in his home country of Japan, the day is called Greenery Day, one of his favorite days. It is held on May 4. There, as in the United States, the day is celebrated by planting trees.

9   Mr. Agawa took his class outside to the front of the school. The principal was already standing there with three saplings that she bought at a garden center. She said that one day they would grow tall and shade the front of the school.

10   The students worked like ants to plant the trees. They took turns digging the holes and poured rocks into the bottom of each one. Mr. Agawa set a tree into each hole. He held each one straight while students poured the planting soil and lightly patted it down with their hands. The students made sure to fill every hole and pack the soil. This would help the small saplings stand straight as they grew into big trees.

11   When the students went back to the classroom, Aisha asked, "Mr. Agawa, now will you tell us what the pinecones and peanut butter are for?"

12   "Yes, of course," he replied. "We are going to make bird feeders to hang in the large trees behind the school. Just follow the directions on this card."

Pinecone Bird Feeders	
Step 1	Tie a long ribbon around the top of a pinecone for hanging it later.
Step 2	Spread some peanut butter all over the sides of the pinecone.
Step 3	Pour birdseed into a paper plate to cover the plate.
Step 4	Roll the pinecone in the birdseed so the seeds stick to it.
Step 5	Use the ribbon to tie the pinecone to a tree branch.

13   After the students made bird feeders, they hung them in the large trees. A few blue jays and robins flew down and began to peck at the seeds. Aisha now understood the reason for Arbor Day. It is a time to plant new trees and be thankful for older ones.

39   **Based on the suffix -ly, what does _lightly_ mean?**

> He held each one straight while students poured the planting soil and <u>lightly</u> patted it down with their hands.

A   in a way that is light

B   to become light

C   to be light again

D   one who is light

40   **Choose the sentence from the story that BEST supports the conclusion that Mr. Agawa cares about nature.**

A   The students worked like ants to plant the trees.

B   Mr. Agawa pointed out that today was the last Friday in April.

C   Mr. Agawa said that in his home country of Japan, the day is called Greenery Day, one of his favorite days.

D   Her teacher grinned as he answered, "Don't worry, it will all make sense later."

GO ON

Name _____ Date _____

41   **How is the setting important to the story?**

A   Aisha, Caleb, and José are in the same class on Fridays.

B   It is early in the morning and the classrooms are busy.

C   The school principal tells everyone about an important holiday in Japan.

D   The students celebrate a special event by going outside during the school day.

42   **What is the BEST conclusion that can be drawn about the students at the end of the passage?**

A   They did not enjoy planting trees and making bird feeders.

B   They do not understand why it is important to plant trees.

C   They recognize the importance of Arbor Day.

D   They would like to visit Japan.

43   **Which sentence would be BEST to add to Paragraph 10?**

A   It was an unusually hot day.

B   They took turns digging the holes and poured rocks into the bottom of each one.

C   The large oak trees swayed in the breeze.

D   There were many ants crawling around on the ground.

44   **What is the MAIN problem in the beginning of the passage?**

A   Aisha and her classmates want to know why there are unusual items on the activity table.

B   Aisha does not like Mr. Agawa's class.

C   The principal will not allow the students to plant trees.

D   The students do not know how to make bird feeders.

Name _____ Date _____

45 **To make a bird feeder, what step comes BEFORE spreading peanut butter onto the pinecone?**

A   Tie a ribbon around the top of the pinecone.

B   Hang the birdfeeder on a tree.

C   Roll the pinecone in birdseed.

D   Pour birdseed on a plate.

GO ON ▶

Read the poem below and answer the questions that follow.

Sea Star
by Desiya Peterson

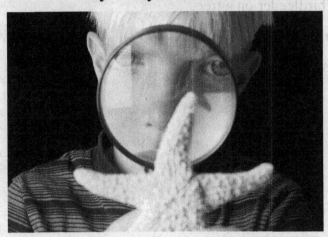

The sea star crawls over the land.

Could it have five arms but not one hand?

It is a star of the ocean,

A wonder of the sea.

5   It is a spiny-skinned creature,

A stanza of poetry.

The sea star has a mouth, but it has no head.

Does it push its stomach from its mouth to be fed?

It is a star of the ocean,

10   A wonder of the sea.

It is a unique creature,

A page out of a fantasy.

One day a predator eats the sea star's arm.

How can the sea star grow it back without a sign of harm?

15   It is a star of the ocean,

A wonder of the sea.

It is a strange creature,

A chapter from a mystery.

46   Which two words from the poem are the MOST SIMILAR in meaning?

      A   land, hand

      B   wonder, mystery

      C   star, ocean

      D   chapter, mystery

47   What does the picture show the reader?

      A   how the sea star's arm grows back

      B   how the sea star is unique

      C   that the boy is curious about the sea star

      D   that the boy does not like the sea star

48   Which of the following lines from the poem contains a metaphor?

      A   The sea star crawls over the land.

      B   The sea star has a mouth, but it has no head.

      C   It is a strange creature,

      D   It is a unique creature, / A page out of a fantasy.

49   Which words from the poem do NOT compare the sea star to literature?

      A   a star of the ocean

      B   a stanza of poetry

      C   a page out of a fantasy

      D   a chapter from a mystery

50   Which identifies "Sea Star" as a poem?

      A   words that describe nature

      B   a beginning and an end

      C   a sentence that compares the sea star to a stanza

      D   lines that end with rhyming words

GO ON

51 **Why did the author MOST LIKELY write "Sea Star"?**

    A   to teach readers about fantasy and mystery books

    B   to persuade readers to collect sea stars

    C   to entertain readers with thoughts about sea stars

    D   to explain how sea stars and poets are alike

Read the passage below and answer the questions that follow.

Power from Wind and Water

1   In the United States, we depend on fossil fuels—fuels that are formed in the earth from plant and animal remains—for most of our energy needs. Fossil fuels include coal and oil, which release harmful gases into the air when burned. We burn them to heat our homes and run our cars. We also burn them to make electricity. We use electricity for lighting, heating, and generating power to run machines.

2   We do not have to depend on fossil fuels to make all of our electrical power, however. We can also get energy from water and wind. Both wind and water are renewable energy sources. Renewable means that we will not use them up because we do not burn them or destroy them to get power from them.

3   Moving water contains energy. We can turn this energy into electricity. One way to do this is by building dams. Dams are strong walls that hold back large amounts of water or control how much water flows in a particular place. When water that has been allowed to collect behind the wall finally gets high enough to go over the dam, it falls with great power. The farther it falls and the more of it there is, the more speed and energy the water has. The powerful moving water runs through pipes to a power station. It makes motors spin inside the power station. The motors then make electricity.

4   Although water power does not pollute the environment, it can have some bad effects. For example, dams can disturb fish by changing their habitats, sometimes causing fish to die. Dams can also put some dry land under water, affecting the habitats of other plants and animals.

5   Wind power is another clean way of making electricity. Getting energy from wind does not pollute the air. We can get power from the wind in much the same way that we get power from water. Wind can make electricity because it is moving. Moving air turns the blades of wind machines. The blades are connected to a drive shaft, which is a long pole that spins when the blades turn. The drive shaft then powers a generator. This generator makes electricity.

6   People often build wind farms, which are places where many wind machines are used together to create energy. Some of the best wind farms are on open, flat land. Others are at the tops of hills or near seashores. Either way, wind is one of the best renewable energy sources.

GO ON

52   Which detail from the passage supports the idea that water power can have some bad effects?

A   Powerful moving water runs through pipes to a power station.

B   Dams hold back large amounts of water.

C   Moving water contains energy.

D   Dams can disturb fish by changing their habitats.

53   What is ONE effect of burning fossil fuels to make energy?

A   They release harmful gases into the air.

B   They can be easily renewed.

C   They help conserve water and other resources.

D   They help plant and animal habitats.

54   Which detail from the passage is an OPINION?

A   Moving water contains energy.

B   Either way, wind is one of the best renewable energy sources.

C   Moving air turns the blades of wind machines.

D   Wind can make electricity because it is moving.

55   Which source would provide the MOST reliable information on renewable energy?

A   a story about a man chasing windmills

B   a student Web page about a class's science experiment

C   a television commercial about wind power

D   an online encyclopedia

Read the speech below and answer the questions that follow.

Camping Club

1   Good morning, young campers! My name is Victoria Moore. As many of you know, I am a fourth grade student here at North Hill Elementary School. I am also the student representative of the North Hill Camping Club. Tomorrow afternoon we will leave for the first camping trip of the year. Please listen carefully as I remind you of a few rules that will help every camper be considerate of nature.

2   First, we must all be careful with our food. Food can cause the most trouble with wild animals. Being careful with food can make the difference between a pleasant camping trip and a frightening one. Our teachers and parents will bring food for a cookout, but many of you might want to bring snacks. If you do, ask your parents to help you pack your food in airtight bags. Airtight bags make it harder for animals to smell your food, so they will be less likely to come into the campsite looking for it.

3   Second, we all need to dispose of our trash properly. Do not expect anyone else to clean up after you. When you leave, carry your trash out with you. Don't leave anything behind. Plastic bags, cans, and other pieces of garbage can be harmful to the health of plants and animals. Let's all remind each other to throw away or recycle our items. We are going camping to observe the beauty of nature, not to destroy it.

4   Third, be prepared to have fun! We'll play games, sing songs, and enjoy the great outdoors. We will also spend some time exploring nature. Bring your magnifying glass, pencil, plant guide, and notebook. You can find interesting plants and identify them using your magnifying glass and plant guide. You might even draw the plant in a notebook and record its name. Remember to check your plant guide if you have forgotten what poison ivy and other dangerous plants look like.

5   It's also very important that each of us stays with our group leader. Each group will have a parent or teacher leader. They will help us pitch our tents, cook our food, and participate in all the fun camping activities. Group leaders will track where we are, so sticking with them will keep you from getting lost. Let's show the group leaders that we kids know how to be kind and considerate campers. Don't forget that the group that has the best behavior and wins the most field day events will win special prizes!

6   Thank you for listening, and I'll see you tomorrow. Please pay attention as Ms. Amado assigns our group leaders.

GO ON

56 Victoria is organizing her note cards with the speaking points she will mention in her speech. What information belongs on the blank note card?

| Introduction | Remind students to be careful with food. | | Remind students to bring a magnifying glass and plant guide. |

A Introduce Ms. Amado to assign group leaders.

B Remind students about the prizes they can win.

C Tell students to clean up their trash.

D Remind students that tomorrow will be the first camping trip of the year.

57 Which source should Victoria use to find a synonym for the underlined word?

> I am also the student <u>representative</u> of the North Hill Camping Club.

A an atlas

B a newspaper

C a thesaurus

D an online encyclopedia

58 Which of the following would BEST improve Victoria's presentation?

A a digital presentation that lists the rules she mentions

B photographs of the students in the camping club

C an audio recording of an interview with recycling expert

D a map of different campsites in the United States

59 **What should students in the audience do while listening to Victoria's speech?**

   A   ask questions before the speech is complete

   B   sit quietly and pay close attention

   C   find a better place to sit if it is hard to see

   D   watch the teacher to know when the speech is over

60 **What is the meaning of the underlined word in the sentence from Paragraph 5?**

   > Group leaders will <u>track</u> where we are, so sticking with
   > them will keep you from getting lost.

   A   to follow a course or trail

   B   footprints made by animals

   C   a line of rails

   D   a place to go running

61 **Which sentence from the speech BEST shows that it is written for a young audience?**

   A   Second, we all need to dispose of our trash properly.

   B   We will also spend some time exploring nature.

   C   My name is Victoria Moore.

   D   Let's show the group leaders that we kids know how to be kind and considerate campers.

GO ON ▶

62 **Which word from the speech BEST completes the analogy?**

> Harmful is to dangerous as considerate is to _____.

   A   interesting

   B   kind

   C   participate

   D   frightening

63 **What is the BEST summary for the speech?**

   A   Students need to learn how to clean up after themselves while camping.

   B   A new camping club will help students enjoy nature.

   C   Everyone should follow the rules during tomorrow's camping trip.

   D   Airtight bags make it harder for animals to smell your food.

The passage below is a rough draft of a biography written for class. It contains mistakes. Read the passage and answer the questions that follow.

Mahalia Jackson

1   Mahalia Jackson was born October 26 1911, in New Orleans, Louisiana. Mahalia, who's grandfather was a slave, was raised by her aunt. Mahalia loved music as a child, and she heard hymns, jazz, and the blues all around her when she was growing up.

2   In 1928, Mahalia moved to Chicago to find new opportunities. _____, she began singing in church choirs. By the 1930s, Mahalia is becoming well known as a gospel singer. By the 1950s, she was singing on radio and TV shows. Mahalia died of heart failure. As the years went on, her popularity continued to grow.

3   In August of 1963, Dr. Martin Luther King, Jr. asked Mahalia to sing at the March on Washington, right before his famous "I Have a Dream" speech. Writing about gospel music in her autobiography, Mahalia said, "It will last as long as any music because it is sung straight from the human heart." At the march, she sang for a crowd of 250,000 people. There are not many singers as loved and honored as Mahalia.

64   Which is the BEST word to add on the blank line?

In 1928, Mahalia moved to Chicago to find new opportunities.
_____, she began singing in church choirs.

A   Soon

B   Although

C   In conclusion

D   Before

65 Which sentence does NOT belong in Paragraph 2?

A In 1928, Mahalia moved to Chicago to find new opportunities.

B By the 1950s, she was singing on radio and TV shows.

C Mahalia died of heart failure.

D As the years went on, her popularity continued to grow.

66 Which is the correct way to write the underlined word?

> Mahalia, who's grandfather was a slave, was raised by her aunt.

A whoose

B whose

C who is

D whos

67 The sentence from the draft has an error in the predicate. Which of the sentences is written correctly?

> By the 1930s, Mahalia is becoming well known as a gospel singer.

A By the 1930s, Mahalia becoming well known as a gospel singer.

B By the 1930s, Mahalia have become well known as a gospel singer.

C By the 1930s, Mahalia was becoming well known as a gospel singer.

D By the 1930s, Mahalia had becoming well known as a gospel singer.

68 Which of these words from the report is a compound word?

A becoming

B singing

C opportunities

D grandfather

69   Choose the BEST order for these sentences from Paragraph 3.

> 1. In August of 1963, Dr. Martin Luther King, Jr. asked Mahalia to sing at the March on Washington, right before his famous "I Have a Dream" speech.
>
> 2. Writing about gospel music in her autobiography, Mahalia said, "It will last as long as any music because it is sung straight from the human heart."
>
> 3. At the march, she sang for a crowd of 250,000 people.

A   3, 1, 2

B   1, 3, 2

C   2, 3, 1

D   3, 2, 1

70   Which is the BEST way to correct this sentence?

> Mahalia Jackson was born October 26 1911, in New Orleans, Louisiana.

A   Mahalia Jackson was born October, 26, 1911, in New Orleans, Louisiana.

B   Mahalia Jackson was born October, 26 1911, in New Orleans, Louisiana.

C   Mahalia Jackson was born October 26, 1911, in New Orleans, Louisiana.

D   Mahalia Jackson was born October 26, 1911, in New Orleans Louisiana.

GO ON ▶

71   Which is the BEST way to make the statement a complete sentence?

> Last year, joined the chorus.

A   I joined last year the chorus.

B   Joined the chorus last year.

C   I last year joined the chorus.

D   Last year, I joined the chorus.

72   Which sentence is written correctly?

> The black cat with green eyes.

A   The black cat with long whiskers and green eyes.

B   The black cat with green eyes quickly.

C   The black cat with green eyes ran quickly.

D   The black cat with green eyes and long tail.

73   Which sentence uses a comma correctly?

A   Jenny brought markers crayons, and paper to school.

B   Jenny brought markers, crayons, and paper to school.

C   Jenny brought markers crayons and, paper to school.

D   Jenny brought markers crayons and paper to school.

74 **What is the correct way to write the underlined words as a contraction?**

Kara <u>does not</u> want to miss the class field trip.

A   don't

B   do'nt

C   does'nt

D   doesn't

75 **Which is a type of story that is usually written to teach a moral or lesson?**

A   tall tale

B   biography

C   personal narrative

D   fable

STOP

Writing to Narrate

Performance Task

Read the text below. Then complete the task that follows.

A Magical Day

Beep! Beep! Beep! As the alarm grew louder, Brianna thought, "I just wish I could sleep a little longer."

Brianna pulled back the covers and forced herself out of bed. Half asleep, she weaved her way through the obstacle course of clothing, books, and toys, and turned off the alarm. But something wasn't quite right. She had an odd sensation, like she wasn't walking at all. Brianna looked down and realized that her feet were not touching the ground. She had not walked across the room—she had flown across. Brianna was flying!

Brianna's heart beat louder and faster. She couldn't believe what was happening, but she loved it. She wanted to see if she could fly to the bathroom. First she had to make sure no one was in the hall. She didn't want to be discovered just yet.

Brianna opened her door quietly and peeked around the doorway. No one was there. It was safe. She quickly flew to the bathroom. It worked! Now it was time to have some real fun. She was going to fly downstairs and surprise her family. She smiled just thinking about all the things that she would be able to do that day. This was going to be a magical day.

In the story, Brianna discovers that she has a special power. Think about what might happen to Brianna throughout the day, at home with her family and at school with her friends.

Write an ending for the story by describing what happens to Brianna. Use this space to plan your writing. Write your ending on a separate sheet of paper.

Planning

_____

_____

STOP

Writing to Inform

Performance Task

Read the text below. Then complete the task that follows.

How to Study for Tests

Are you good at taking tests? Some students are, but others really struggle. Here are some strategies to help you do well on tests.

Plan Ahead

Once you find out you are going to have a test, make a plan. Mark a calendar for times to study a little bit each day. For example, suppose you find out on Monday that you will have a spelling test on Friday. You might decide to study a few new words each evening. It is important to set aside some time each day to study.

Find a Quiet Place

Study in a quiet place that has as few distractions as possible. That might be your bedroom, the back porch, the library, or a park. It can be lots of places, but it's definitely NOT in front of the television.

Study Together

Sometimes it helps to study with a partner. For a spelling test, one person could say the words aloud while the other writes them down. If something that you're studying is confusing, you can figure it out together. If you still don't understand it, be sure to ask the teacher.

The text describes a task—how to study for tests. Think about how the headings in the text help organize the passage.

Think about a task that you do. It might be a chore at home or a job at school. Write an informative essay to explain the task and how to do it. Plan and write your essay on separate sheets of paper.

STOP

Georgia Test Power
130
Grade 4, Writing Practice Test

Writing Opinions

Performance Task

Read the two letters to the editor that follow. Take notes on each text. After you read, follow the directions to write an essay about what you have read.

For Bike Lanes

Dear Mayor Thompson,

I understand that the City Council will be discussing bike lanes next week. I want to let you know that I am in favor of them. There are many reasons I feel this way.

1. We need bike lanes for safety. More and more people are riding bikes these days. Without bike lanes, more people will be riding bikes on the crowded sidewalks. Also, people will ride bikes in the streets anyway. It will be much safer to have lanes along the side of the street just for bikes.

2. More bike lanes will help reduce pollution in our community. That's because bike lanes will encourage more people to ride bikes instead of drive cars. That will result in less pollution from cars.

3. Bicycles are cheap compared with cars. If more people ride bikes instead of drive cars, they will save money on car repairs and gasoline.

4. Fewer cars will help ease the traffic jams and the parking problem downtown. However, we'll need to have more bike racks set up downtown, at shopping malls, and other places. These are fairly inexpensive.

In conclusion, I support adding bike lanes to our streets as soon as possible. This change will improve our community for everyone. Thank you for your time.

Which reason for adding bike lanes is the most convincing to you?

_____

_____

_____

GO ON ▶

Name _____ Date _____

Against Bike Lanes

Dear Mayor Thompson,

There has been a movement in our town to make bike lanes on our streets. I think we should take the money that would be used for the bike lanes and use it to build a new park instead. I like to ride a bike as much as anyone. However, I think that a new park would be more beneficial to everyone.

The main reason I am against bike lanes is that I think they are dangerous. It is much safer to ride a bicycle on a path in a park than it is to ride on a road with cars. Many of our roads are dangerous enough for the car drivers with all of the traffic that we have.

Another reason I want to build a park instead of bike lanes is to avoid all of the delays caused by the construction of bike lanes. Some roads may need to be closed in order to widen the street. Some roads will not be widened. But they will still need to be closed while the bike lanes are painted.

Finally, I believe that a park would benefit everyone in the community, not just people who ride bikes. A park could have open spaces, a playground, and trails for walking and biking. Thank you for your time.

Why does this writer think bike lanes are dangerous?

_____

_____

You have read two different opinions about bike lanes. Write an essay explaining your opinion about bike lanes. Cite evidence from the two letters to support your opinion, but give additional reasons. Use this space to help you plan your writing. Write your essay on a separate sheet of paper.

Planning

_____

_____

Writing and Research

Performance Task

Read the two texts that follow. Take notes on each one. After you read, follow the directions to write an essay about what you have read.

Musical Instruments in Africa

Music is an important part of cultures around the world. People use instruments to create rhythm, tell stories, and express emotions. Examples include some instruments in different parts of Africa. You can group instruments from Africa and elsewhere by the way they create sound. There are four categories of instruments.

Aerophones are instruments that create sound when a person blows air through them. Examples from Africa include flutes, whistles, trumpets, and horns.

Chordophones create sound when a string is plucked or strummed or even when a bow is run across the strings. Some African examples of this type of instrument are the zither, lyre, harp, and folk lute.

Membranophones have a skin or other thin material stretched over a sound box. Drums are probably the most familiar membranophone. In a drum, the sound is created when the musician hits the thin material with a hand, a stick, or some other object. Another way to create sound with this type of instrument is to blow on the membrane. That's how a kazoo works.

Idiophones make sounds when the instrument is shaken or moved. Examples from Africa include bells, clappers, rattles, gongs, and xylophones.

These are just a few of the many musical instruments that people use to express themselves through music.

How is an idiophone different from a chordophone?

_____

_____

GO ON ▶

Musical Instruments in the Orchestra

An orchestra has many different instruments, but they can all be grouped into four categories. These categories are strings, woodwinds, brass, and percussion.

More than half of the orchestra's instruments are strings. They make sounds when strings are plucked or tapped. Examples include the violin, viola, cello, double bass, and harp. The harp is the only one of these instruments that does not have a hollow wooden body.

Woodwinds are instruments that create sound when the musician blows air into them. The musician can change the sounds by pressing on different keys while blowing into the instrument. A long time ago these instruments were made of wood. Today, most of them are made of metal. Woodwinds include the flute, oboe, clarinet, and bassoon.

The loudest instruments in the orchestra are the brass instruments. Sound is created by vibrating the lips over a mouthpiece. The brass instruments in the orchestra are the French horn, trumpet, trombone, and tuba.

Percussion instruments create sound when they are hit, shaken, or scraped. Examples include the snare drum, timpani, and cymbals.

The next time you hear a school band or orchestra, listen for the different types of instruments. Be sure to also appreciate how the different sounds work together to create something marvelous.

What is the main difference in the way that brass instruments and woodwinds create sound?

_____

_____

You have read two texts about different ways to group musical instruments. Think about the information that each presents. Reread all or parts of the texts as needed.

Write an essay that describes how you would group all of the instruments you have read about. Plan and write your final essay on separate sheets of paper. Remember to use textual evidence to support your ideas.

STOP

Name _____ Date _____

Reading/Writing Practice Test

Read the passage below and answer the questions that follow.

Tell the World

1   The planet is inhabited by many people. Each person shares a responsibility for it. What can a person do if he or she finds something that needs to be changed in how people treat the planet or each other?

2   Severn Suzuki was a 12-year-old girl who lived in Vancouver, Canada. Severn had always enjoyed nature. She loved going camping and fishing. One day she went fishing with her dad and learned that the fish were full of cancers.

3   Severn began to worry about the environment. She worried about plants and animals. She also worried about other problems that the world faced, such as children who were going hungry. Severn knew she had to do something.

4   She became a member of the Environmental Children's Organization (ECO). This group of 12- and 13-year-olds from Canada wanted to stop the destruction of the environment and make the world a better place. Group members wanted to keep the world safe for future generations.

5   The group raised money to travel 6,000 miles (9,654 kilometers) to the Earth Summit in Rio de Janeiro, Brazil. Members planned to speak before the United Nations Conference on Environment and Development.

6   More than 100 leaders and members of environmental organizations were at this meeting. They wanted to figure out how to save plants and animals. Many plants and animals were disappearing and in danger of becoming extinct.

7   Severn Suzuki was one of the four children who spoke at the conference. In her speech, she shared her biggest fears:

8   "Losing my future is not like losing an election or a few points on the stock market. I am here to speak for all generations to come.

9   I am here to speak on behalf of the starving children around the world whose cries go unheard.

10   I am here to speak for the countless animals dying across this planet because they have nowhere left to go. We cannot afford to be unheard.

11   I am afraid to go out in the sun now because of the holes in the ozone. I am afraid to breathe the air because I don't know what chemicals are in it.

GO ON ▶

12   I used to go fishing in Vancouver with my dad until just a few years ago when we found the fish full of cancers. And now we hear about animals and plants going extinct every day—vanishing forever.

13   In my life, I have dreamt of seeing the great herds of wild animals, jungles and rain forests full of birds and butterflies, but now I wonder if they will even exist for my children to see.

14   Did you have to worry about these little things when you were my age?

15   All this is happening before our eyes, and yet we act as if we have all the time we want and all the solutions.

16   I'm only a child and I don't have all the solutions, but I want you to realize neither do you!"

17   She begged the leaders, "If you don't know how to fix it, please stop breaking it!" Severn reminded them, "We are all in this together and should act as one single world working toward one single goal."

18   Many people were moved by Severn Suzuki's speech. She told the world exactly how she felt. That was the first step to making a difference.

1   **Based on the author's description of Severn Suzuki, what can the reader conclude about Suzuki's personality? Give TWO details from the passage to support your answer.**

_____

_____

_____

_____

_____

2   What is the meaning of the word *environment* as it is used in Paragraph 3? Use text evidence to support your answer.

_____

_____

_____

_____

3   Complete the web with ONE detail from the passage.

Severn's Fears

Animals are dying because they have no place left to go.

Animals and plants are going extinct every day.

Explain how this detail is important. Use evidence from the text.

_____

_____

_____

_____

GO ON ▶

4   According to the author, what does it take for someone to help the world?
    Use evidence from the text to support your answer.

_____

_____

_____

_____

Name _____ Date _____

Unit 2
PRACTICE TEST

Unit 2
PRACTICE TEST

Reading/Writing Practice Test

Read the passage below and answer the questions that follow.

Time Out

1 "Maria, will you play with me?"

2 I glanced up from my book to see my little sister Sasha standing by my chair. Sighing, I shut the book, keeping my thumb between the pages to mark my place. I didn't want to hurt Sasha's feelings, but it was already past four o'clock and I didn't have time.

3 "I'm in the middle of this book, sweetie," I said gently, "and then I have some homework to do before dinner, and I have basketball practice after that. Maybe we can play tomorrow."

4 "I don't want to play with you tomorrow," said Sasha flatly. "I want to play with you *now*."

5 "You could build with your blocks," I suggested. "That's a fun thing to do by yourself." I tried to sound jolly and enthusiastic, but I knew I was fighting a losing battle.

6 "Blocks are boring," said Sasha. "Anyway, the blocks are in time out because I tried to build a tower but it fell down and squished my foot, so I put the blocks in time out, just like Mommy does to me when I do something bad."

7 I had to smile at the idea of putting blocks in time out. Sasha gets put in time out—well, not all the time, but it does happen fairly often, so I guess she knows what it's like.

8 "Maria, I want to play with you," Sasha repeated.

9 I closed my eyes and rubbed my forehead. The trouble with Sasha—well, there are lots of troubles with Sasha, but one is that she doesn't ever believe you when you say no to her, or at least, she doesn't accept it when you say it. Instead, she just stands there asking you again and again until you finally agree to do exactly what she wants.

10 "I really really really really want you to play with me," Sasha said.

11 I glanced down at my book and sighed again. "I guess this can wait while we play for a bit," I said.

12 "We're going to play with my stuffed animals," Sasha explained as I walked into her room.

13 I sat down next to Monkeykins, one of Sasha's favorites. "Let's see what Monkeykins wants to do today."

GO ON

14   "Oh, you can't play with Monkeykins," Sasha informed me. "She's in time out."

15   I looked quizzically at Sasha. "What did she do to get herself into time out?"

16   "Something *terrible*," Sasha said in a low voice, her eyes as big as dinner plates. "She pulled Elephant's tail."

17   Inside I was laughing, but I pretended to be shocked.

18   "She pulled it," Sasha repeated, "and Elephant cried and I put Monkeykins in time out and she has to stay there until she's ready to behave."

19   "Did you hear what just happened, Maria?"

20   I looked up from the stuffed raccoon I was holding.

21   "Bubbles was being mean to Sparky," Sasha explained sorrowfully. She picked up a stuffed pig and shook her finger in its face. "That was very naughty, Bubbles," she said. "It's not nice to call people nasty names, so I'm going to need to put you in time out."

22   I stifled a laugh. Time out was growing larger and larger every minute; besides Monkeykins, Sasha had put a sheep, a bear, a parrot, a moose, and two rabbits in time out in just the last ten minutes, and now it looked like Bubbles the pig was going to join them. I playfully threw Bubbles into the time-out pile.

23   "Maria! That's not very nice to do to Bubbles," Sasha said seriously. "I'm sorry, but you'll have to go in time out, too."

24   This time I couldn't help laughing out loud. Sasha led me to time out. At least I would get to play with Monkeykins now.

1   **What are Maria's feelings toward Sasha? Give TWO details from the passage to support your answer.**

_____

_____

_____

_____

2   What does Maria's mother mean when she compares Sasha to rain falling on a rock? Use text evidence to support your answer.

_____

_____

_____

_____

3   What do you learn about Sasha in the passage? Give TWO details from the passage to support your answer.

_____

_____

_____

_____

GO ON ▶

Name _____ Date _____

Unit 2
PRACTICE TEST

Common Core
Reading/Writing

Unit 2
PRACTICE TEST

Common Core
Reading/Writing

4 Think about the order of events in the passage.

Complete the timeline with ONE detail from the passage.

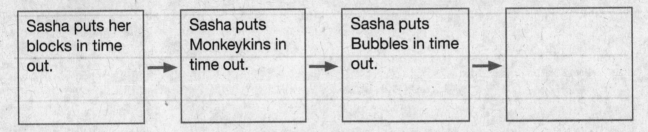

Sasha puts her blocks in time out.	→	Sasha puts Monkeykins in time out.	→	Sasha puts Bubbles in time out.	→	

Explain why this detail is important. Use evidence from the text.

_____

_____

_____

_____

_____

STOP

Reading/Writing Practice Test

Read the passage below and answer the questions that follow.

Garden Show Opens Soon

1   GREEN VALLEY August 8— In just one short week, our annual Green Valley Amazing Vegetables Garden Show begins. Just like every year, we are looking forward to our favorite Green Valley event. This year's show promises to be better than ever. It will be held on August 15 at the Green Valley City Park.

2   The event will kick off with the Amazing Vegetables Parade. The parade starts at City Hall at 8:00 A.M. and marches on Spring Street to the park. (See schedule of events at the end of this article.) The parade features more than 100 farmers and gardeners pushing wheelbarrows filled with their amazing vegetables. The judges will award a prize for the best-decorated wheelbarrow. The Green Valley High School marching band is also scheduled to appear in the parade, along with several marching scout groups.

3   Morning events include the Tomato and Pepper Contest and the Squash and Onions Contest. Last year, Dr. W. D. Seeds grew the largest tomato ever seen in Green Valley. It weighed in at 8 pounds, 4 ounces. Will anyone tie or break her record this year? Will anyone grow a pepper hotter than Sammy Ortega's winner from last year? Visit the Tomato and Pepper Tent to find out.

4   People visiting the Squash and Onions Tent are in for some grand sights. Last year, it took two people to lift some of the squashes, including—of course—the prizewinner. The biggest onion was nearly the size of a soccer ball! Ribbons will be awarded for the largest squash and onion.

5   Be sure to stop by the baseball field for lunch. Have a slice of vegetable lasagna made by students from Green Valley School. They are going for a world record for the longest dish of lasagna. Iced vegetable drinks and corn on the cob will also be served.

GO ON

6   The Carrots and Corn Contest will be held in the afternoon, with prizes awarded at 4:00 P.M. The Tanner twins took the prizes last year for the biggest carrot and the biggest ear of corn. One carrot was almost as tall as the twins! Can they do it again? Come see for yourself!

7   Two other events are sure to draw crowds all day. Both the Vegetables-on-View Tent and our own Farmers' Market will be open to the public from 9:00 A.M. until 5:00 P.M. A contest called *That Vegetable Looks Just Like . . .* will invite growers with a good imagination. The contest will be held at the Vegetables-on-View Tent. Last year, Daisy Black grew a pumpkin that looked just like her dog, Spot. Mr. Lee from Lee's Hardware Store grew a potato that looked like Benjamin Franklin. Both won prizes. You never know what will turn up in this popular contest.

8   The Farmers' Market will sell the most amazing vegetables. Most are huge, and all are delicious. Shoppers are advised to bring their wheelbarrows and load up on vegetables. Free delivery is offered for those who buy a truckload.

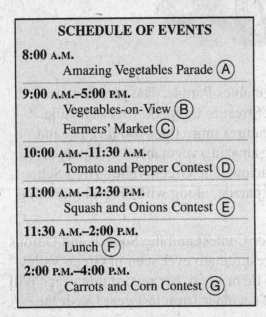

SCHEDULE OF EVENTS

8:00 A.M.
    Amazing Vegetables Parade (A)

9:00 A.M.–5:00 P.M.
    Vegetables-on-View (B)
    Farmers' Market (C)

10:00 A.M.–11:30 A.M.
    Tomato and Pepper Contest (D)

11:00 A.M.–12:30 P.M.
    Squash and Onions Contest (E)

11:30 A.M.–2:00 P.M.
    Lunch (F)

2:00 P.M.–4:00 P.M.
    Carrots and Corn Contest (G)

1   How does the reader know that the author is trying to persuade readers to visit the Garden Show? Give TWO details from the passage to support your answer.

_____

_____

_____

_____

2   How is the information in the passage organized? Use evidence from the text to support your answer.

_____

_____

_____

_____

GO ON ▶

3 Think about the information provided in the passage. Complete the idea support map to support the idea that the Garden Show is full of unusual things to see.

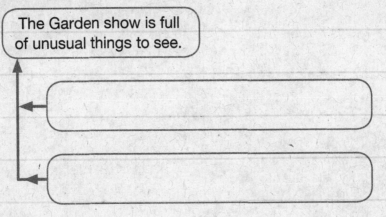

The Garden show is full of unusual things to see.

Explain why these two details are important. Use evidence from the text.

_____

_____

_____

_____

_____

4 How could the reader use the information in the text, schedule, and map to plan a visit to the Garden Show? Use text evidence to support your answer.

_____

_____

_____

_____

_____

STOP

Reading/Writing Practice Test

Read the play below and answer the questions that follow.

Lost and Found

Characters:

JON LIU, age 9

ANDREW LIU, age 11

MRS. LIU

BETHANY THOMAS, age 16

MR. THOMAS

SCENE 1

(*Jon and Andrew enter from stage left, carrying backpacks and wearing school clothes.*)

JON: Did you see that kickball game at recess? (*Stops walking and holds up his hand, listening.*) Hold on, did you hear something?

ANDREW: Yeah, it sounded like a bell, and I think it was coming from over here. (*Andrew walks to a bush, reaches behind it, and picks up a kitten with a bell on its collar.*)

JON: What are you doing back there, little guy? (*Takes the kitten from Andrew.*) Andrew, do you think we can keep him? Mom said maybe we could get a cat sometime soon, and I bet that if we ask really, really nicely, she'll say we can have this one!

ANDREW: Let's go home and we can see what she says.

(*Andrew and Jon exit stage right.*)

SCENE 2

(*Jon is sitting on the living room floor, petting the kitten while Andrew watches. Mrs. Liu walks in and jumps, startled.*)

MRS. LIU: Where did that kitten come from?

ANDREW: We found it behind some bushes down at the other end of the street.

JON: (*Jumps up and runs over to his mother, eager.*) Can we keep it?

MRS. LIU: (*Walks over and picks up the kitten, looking thoughtful.*) It has a collar, so that suggests that someone is taking care of it. It probably ran outside and got lost, so I imagine that the owner must be looking for it.

GO ON ▶

JON: *(Looks disappointed, then perks up.)* But if it turns out that no one is trying to find it, then we can keep it, right?

MRS. LIU: *(Hands the kitten to Jon, who hugs it close.)* Well, let's try to find the owner first. Why don't you boys make posters to put up in the neighborhood? I'll put an advertisement in the newspaper tomorrow, and if no one claims the kitten, then maybe we'll keep it.

ANDREW: I'll get some paper and markers.

SCENE 3

(The boys are outside finishing up taping a poster to a telephone pole. As they walk away, Bethany and Mr. Thomas walk toward the pole, looking from side to side and calling for a cat.)

BETHANY: Simon! Here, kitty, kitty, kitty! *(She pauses and frowns.)* Aw, Dad, we'll never find him! I really wish I'd closed the back door!

MR. THOMAS: Well, let's just keep looking. He's probably still nearby. *(Stops in front of the poster and starts to read it.)* Hey, look. "Did you lose a cute little—"

BETHANY: *(She turns to look at the sign and clasps her hands together under her chin.)* Oh, Dad, do you think it might be—

JON *(Starts to speak, then hesitates as Bethany and Mr. Thomas turn to look at him, then starts again)*: Um, are you looking for an orange kitten? One that's real nice and doesn't scratch you when you pick him up?

BETHANY: *(Excited.)* Dad, I bet that's Simon!

ANDREW: The kitten was hiding behind some bushes, and we found him when we were walking home. Come on, we'll show you. *(Andrew starts to walk away. Jon doesn't follow, and looks sad.)* Jon, come on! This girl has to be his owner.

JON: *(To Andrew, in a low voice; Bethany is watching them and overhears.)* I bet she really misses her cat, but now I'll never see him again!

BETHANY: We live right in the neighborhood, so you could visit him sometimes. He always needs someone to play with while I do my homework.

JON: Really? Wow! You bet I'll come visit!

(All walk offstage.)

1   What features does this play include that would NOT be found in a story?

_____

_____

_____

_____

_____

2   Complete the Venn diagram with details from the play. Show how Jon's and
Andrew's reactions to the kitten are alike and different.

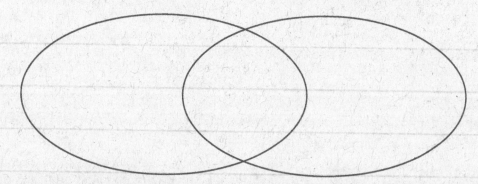

Jon's Reactions   Andrew's Reactions

Explain how Jon's and Andrew's reactions to the kitten are alike and different.
Use evidence from the text to support your answer.

_____

_____

_____

_____

GO ON ▶

Name _____ Date _____

3   Suppose you are playing the part of Bethany in a production of "Lost and
    Found." What emotions would you use while reading your lines in the
    beginning of Scene 3? Use text evidence to support your answer.

_____

_____

_____

_____

4   What lesson does Jon learn in the play? Give TWO details from the play to
    support your answer.

_____

_____

_____

_____

STOP

Reading/Writing Practice Test

Read the passages below and answer the questions that follow.

Inventing the Telephone

1   Suppose that you want to talk to your friend who lives across the street without leaving your house. You could yell to your friend, but you would have to yell loudly. On the other hand, you could use the telephone to speak to your friend directly. You could even talk to someone on the other side of the world with a telephone. Where did this powerful machine come from?

2   Today telephones are a part of everyday life. But 150 years ago, no one had ever seen one. People who wanted to send messages over long distances used the telegraph. The telegraph used electricity to send messages. Changes in electric current stood for the letters of the alphabet. Telegraph wires carried messages hundreds or even thousands of miles.

3   Alexander Graham Bell studied how the telegraph worked. From childhood, he was interested in sounds and human speech. His father was a well-known expert on speech, and his mother was unable to hear. As a young man, Bell worked as a teacher for students who were deaf. He worked in his spare time to make a better telegraph.

4   Since more and more telegraph messages were being sent over telegraph wires, Bell wanted to create a new telegraph that could send many messages at the same time. Bell thought that his telegraph would use different pitches of sound to keep the various messages in order.

5   Bell worked with an assistant, Thomas Watson, to perfect his new telegraph. One day, while they worked on their project, Bell made an accidental discovery. He learned that electricity could carry sound directly. He decided to work on a machine that would send the sound of a person's voice from one place to another.

GO ON ▶

Name _____ Date _____

6   Bell and Watson worked on the telephone for many months. Their basic idea was correct, but they were unable to make the sound easy to understand. Then on February 14, 1876, Bell announced to the U.S. government that he had found a way to send the human voice over wires. But the world's first telephone call happened a few weeks later. Bell made the call on March 10 to his assistant, saying, "Mr. Watson, come here. I want you." That summer, he introduced his new invention to the world at the Philadelphia Centennial Exposition.

1   What problem did the invention of the telephone help to solve? Give ONE detail from the passage to support your answer.

_____

_____

_____

_____

2   What experiences in Alexander Graham Bell's life led him to invent the telephone? Use text evidence to support your answer.

_____

_____

_____

_____

Talking on a String

At the Save Our Planet Club, we are always looking for new ways to reuse and recycle everyday materials. Here's a fun way you can reuse cans to make a can telephone.

Materials:

- 2 cans, about the same size, clean and empty; each can has one lid removed
- hammer
- nail
- pencil
- string, 8–10 feet long

What To Do:

1. Gather all your materials. Find an adult who can help you.

2. Place your cans on the ground with the open ends facing down. Mark a spot in the center of each top. Then ask the adult to help you punch a hole through the marked spot with a hammer and a nail in the top of each can.

3. Next push one end of the string through the hole in one of the cans. Use a pencil to push the string through, *not your finger*. Then knot the string firmly inside the can.

4. Push the other end of the same string through the hole in the top of the second can and knot it also. Now you have your can telephone.

Using Your Can Telephone:

To enjoy your telephone, find a friend to use it with. Each of you take one can. Pull the string tightly between you and make sure it does not touch anything. Speak into your can while your friend holds the other can to his or her ear. Then switch roles. Teach others how to make can telephones. It can be fun!

How a Can Telephone Works:

Like a real telephone, your can telephone lets sound waves travel back and forth. Sound travels well through a solid, like your piece of string. When one person speaks into the can, the sound makes the string vibrate. The sound waves travel along the string to the other can telephone. When they reach your friend's ear, he or she can hear what you said. What happens if you pinch the string with your finger? The sound waves are interrupted. They cannot travel past your finger. As a result, your friend will not hear what you said. The sound waves cannot reach the other can.

GO ON ▶

3 Imagine you want to tell a friend how to make a can telephone. Write a few
   sentences explaining the process in your own words. Base your answer on
   details in the text.

_____

_____

_____

_____

4 Complete the Venn diagram with details from the passages. Show how
   Alexander Graham Bell's first telephone and a can telephone are alike and
   how they are different.

Alexander Graham Bell's
First Telephone   Can Telephone

   Explain how the two telephones are alike and how they are different.
   Use evidence from both texts to support your answer.

_____

_____

_____

_____

STOP

Reading/Writing Practice Test

Read the folktales below and answer the questions that follow.

Opossum and Iguana

1   Long ago, Opossum lived in a Mexican village. Quiet and watchful, she sat all day in a mango tree and saw everything that was going on in the village. The other animals never noticed her or came to visit.

2   Underneath the mango tree lived Iguana. Iguana was the only villager who knew how to make fire from sticks. When the people in the village needed fire for cooking or warmth, they came to him.

3   One night Opossum heard Iguana say loudly to his wife, "I should be the ruler of this village because I am the only one who can make fire. I will show all the villagers how much they need me!" Then he took all the fire and climbed to the top of a cliff.

4   The next morning the villagers cried out, "There is no fire!"

5   "Iguana carried it up the cliff to the sky," explained Opossum.

6   The villagers discussed who should go to get back the fire. They all agreed that Opossum should go.

7   So Opossum scrambled up the cliff. At the top she found Iguana.

8   "I suppose you've come to steal my fire," said Iguana.

9   Opossum said, "You are too smart for me, Iguana, and I could never steal fire from you."

10   Iguana's chest puffed up, and he began to tell boastful stories about himself. On and on he went, telling one story after another until Opossum said, "You look tired."

11   "I *am* tired," Iguana yawned, and he turned away and fell asleep. As he did, Opossum reached into the fire, wrapped her tail around a burning branch, and threw it over the edge of the cliff to the villagers below. In the process, all the hair on her tail burned away.

12   "You thief!" Iguana shouted, waking up and seeing what she was doing.

GO ON ▶

13   Frightened, Opossum curled up and pretended to be dead. Iguana poked her to see if she was really dead. His poke was so strong that Opossum fell over the side of the cliff. Fortunately, Raven caught her.

14   Now everyone in the village had fire. They no longer had to ask Iguana when they needed fire for cooking or warmth. Still, to this day, Opossum has a hairless tail, which reminds everyone of how she brought fire to the people. And if Opossum is in danger, she continues to curl up into a ball and pretend to be dead.

1   **How does Opossum feel at the beginning of the folktale? Give ONE detail from the folktale to support your answer.**

_____

_____

_____

_____

2   **How did Opossum get the fire from Iguana? Use evidence from the text to support your answer.**

_____

_____

_____

_____

_____

How I Lost My Tail, by Mr. B. Bear

1   This is what happened to me, and I promise you it's the truth, or my name isn't Mr. B. Bear.

2   Long ago, back when I was young, I had a long bushy tail. I was extremely proud of my tail, which was better-looking than any other bear's, if I do say so myself.

3   One bitter winter day I was lumbering along when I ran into Ms. Fox, who just happened to be carrying a whole mess of freshly-caught fish. "Oh, Ms. Fox, ma'am," I said, "please tell me where you got that delicious-looking set of fish."

4   "Why, certainly, Mr. Bear," said Ms. Fox politely, and she gestured toward the north. "If you walk that way," she told me, "you'll see a beautiful lake. Walk out on the ice and find a hole just big enough for your tail. Coat your tail with honey and dip it down into the water. The fish will grab onto your tail and get stuck. Just haul your tail back up when you think you have all the fish you need."

5   "Thank you very much, ma'am," I said.

6   Well, I found the lake just fine. I walked out on the ice, found a hole, and coated my tail with honey. Then I stuck my tail down the hole and sat. Within five minutes I could tell that at least a dozen fish were stuck to my tail. I started to get up, but changed my mind. If a dozen fish were good, then two dozen fish would be better.

7   So I waited till I was pretty sure I had two dozen fish. Then I decided to wait till there were three dozen. Finally, after four dozen fish, my tail was getting awfully cold. So I stood up. Only I couldn't. My tail was stuck tight in the icy clutches of the lake!

8   I began to panic. I couldn't stay there forever! So I gave one mighty heave, and my body got up all right, but my tail stayed right where it was, frozen solid in the ice!

9   And so that's why bears have short stubby tails these days. And that's the truth, or my name isn't Mr. B. Bear!

GO ON ▶

3 **How do the different points of view make the folktales different? Use text
evidence from both texts to support your answer.**

_____

_____

_____

_____

4 **Complete the T Map diagram. Use details from the plots of the two folktales
that show how they are alike and how they are different.**

How Stories are Alike	How Stories are Different

**Explain how the plots of the two folktales are alike and how they are
different. Use evidence from both texts to support your answer.**

_____

_____

_____

_____

STOP